# TAXATION FOR
# SMALL BUSINESSES

# BUSINESS GUIDEBOOKS

## SELF-HELP GUIDES FOR SMALL BUSINESSMEN

# TAXATION FOR SMALL BUSINESSES

## J.G. McCLURE & A.G. LAVIES

### DIRECTORS OF TAX & FINANCIAL PLANNING LIMITED

SERIES FOREWORD BY DAVID TRIPPIER,
UNDER SECRETARY OF STATE AT THE
DEPARTMENT OF INDUSTRY

**Sphere Reference**

Sphere Reference
30/32 Gray's Inn Road
London
WC1X 8JL

First published by
Sphere Books Ltd 1985

Typeset by The Word Factory, Rossendale, Lancashire.
Printed and bound in Great Britain by
Cox & Wyman Ltd, Reading

# CONTENTS

# SERIES FOREWORD

by David Trippier MP,
Parliamentary Under Secretary of State for Industry

---

The environment for small businesses has changed for the better in the past four years. An effective Loan Guarantee Scheme and generous tax relief through the Business Expansion Scheme are only two of many in over 100 Government measures to provide incentives and remove obstacles to business enterprise. Our efforts are complemented by a welcome improvement in attitudes in commerce and industry towards the small business operator.

Vital though these changes are, the success of any new expanding business will always depend on the skill, knowledge and tenacity of those running the firm. Practical sources of expertise and advice, as provided by this series of Business Guidebooks, are invaluable aids for the busy entrepreneur. General business management and finance, without doubt, cause the most problems and biggest headaches for the small firm.

Certainly many young businesses have been given a better chance of success by the increasing availability of help with the particular challenges that beset them. I am encouraged by figures which show for the two years, 1981 and 1982, 'births' of new firms well in excess of 'deaths' in spite of the worldwide economic recession.

A flourishing small firms sector in any national economy brings new energy, new enterprise and new initiatives into industry and commerce. These attributes have never been more necessary than in today's tough economic climate and highly competitive world markets. To this end, these Business Guidebooks will be a worthwhile investment for every new and expanding business.

# INTRODUCTION

This book is not intended to be a textbook giving the intricate details of the United Kingdom Taxation system. As with the other books in this series the aim is to provide an introduction to and explanation of the subject so that you can be in control of your own affairs even if you have to seek professional advice. The book is intended for readers who are considering starting up their own business or who may already be running a small business.

The tax aspects of your business may remain a mystery by neglect. If this is so, then this is one area of your business that is out of control and may produce some unfortunate surprises. Your tax affairs may remain a mystery by your delegation of them to a professional adviser. In this case are you still going to receive surprises? Do you understand enough about the subject to be able to control that adviser or have you just abdicated responsibility?

Taxation in its various forms should be regarded as a business expense. In some cases or in a particular year that expense could be the majority of your own and/or the business' expenditure. If you were buying a new car or even a coffee machine for your office you might spend some time and attention to making the best buy or achieving a 10% discount.

Surely, however busy you may be in running your own business, you should devote some time to understanding what types of tax you and your business have paid, are presently paying and, most important, are likely to pay in the future.

We have worked in the tax departments of accountants practices, in the tax department of an oil company and for the last five years we have been running our own business. Our business is a tax consultancy, which is not a high risk business but we have also ventured into the areas of computer software development and marketing software, which is high risk.

Therefore, in relation to taxation we have been advisers, both from outside and inside businesses. We also have the experience of running our own business and that we hope has provided us with a sense of proportion as to the importance of tax matters.

Your own particular tax problem will not necessarily be solved by reading this book but we hope the book will provide you with an understanding of the tax implications of your business. We also hope it will alert you as to when to find out more or when to seek professional advice. Overall we would like to think this book might dispel any fears you may have about tax and actually give you a positive interest in the subject as it affects yourself and your business.

It is a well-known saying that 'the tax tail should not be allowed to wag the dog'. That is to say that tax advice should not be allowed to dictate personal or business decisions. However almost every business decision has some tax implication and those implications should be understood and taken into account as part of the decision-making process. It is surprising how, even in very large companies, business forecasts, on which decisions are based, are often prepared totally neglecting tax implications or effects.

You often hear in cases of businesses which fail that tax demands were the final blow that brought the business down. This is usually said as if it was totally unexpected to the businessman concerned that the Inland Revenue should ask for such tax payments as were due whereas in fact it should have been predictable and to some extent controllable.

It has been a habit in the UK to treat accounting for businesses as an historic exercise. In cases of sole proprietors (as opposed to limited companies) accounts have only been drawn up for the purposes of settling taxation liabiliites with the Revenue. This function has often been left to an accountant and therefore the business has been conducted on a day to day basis without considering taxation to any great extent. The businessman awaits after the year end the judgement of the accountant as to the amount of tax due.

People are now realising that with computer-based accounting systems and forecasting systems available at quite low costs for both hardware and software there is no longer any excuse for treating accounting as such an historic exercise. However, in bringing the accounting records and forecasting on to a regular monthly basis it would be wrong to ignore the taxation aspects.

Although an understanding of all tax regulations may be difficult to acquire it should be possible for any businessman to acquire sufficient knowledge to understand the major tax aspects of his own business. The tax laws can change and some aspect of the business might involve tax implications which had not previously applied to that business, therefore it would be prudent for the businessman always to have the tax aspects reviewed by a tax advisor.

In this book we have focussed on major decisions which you have to face in setting-up and running a business. We have then tried to explain the relevant tax implications of those decisions.

We wish to thank our secretaries, Yvette Deacon and Angela Fairs, for all their hard work in typing this book which was undertaken on top of their existing heavy workload.

Anne Lavies
Gordon McClure

# 'Background'

This first section of the book describes the U.K. tax system, the relevant authorities and the administrative aspects of the subject.

We have already said that this is not a textbook. Therefore do not expect to be able to dip into these pages to find a specific answer to your own problem. There are plenty of tax guides available to help you there. You may understand very well a tax problem which you know relates to your business, but how many tax problems does your business have of which you are not aware?

We hope this 'background' section might help you identify all the tax aspects of your business leaving you to seek answers to specific points raised, by reason of your increased knowledge.

# 1. What is Tax? — understanding the animal in its many and varied forms

Forget for the moment the role of the Inland Revenue and Customs & Excise. They act only as agents in assessing and collecting tax on behalf of the Government.

Taxation is a basic part of Government economic policy. The privilege of living and working in the United Kingdom has a price and that is represented by taxation exacted by laws enacted by Parliament.

You may be excused for assuming that the taxes are just a collection of random laws. There is usually some logical reasoning behind the introduction of new tax rules. Sometimes, of course subsequent events occur which defeat the original objectives then these laws can seem ridiculous or unfair.

You need to remember that simplicity and fairness in the tax system cannot always go hand in hand. The simpler a tax system becomes, for example one single rate of tax, then the less fair it may be because it favours the rich to the detriment of the less well off.

The structure of the tax system is based on two basic concepts.

1. The main purpose of taxation is to fund Government expenditure.
2. The burden of tax can be varied as between individuals or businesses to provide incentives. Thus the structure of the tax system can encourage taxpayers to take a certain course of action which the Government wants to encourage as a part of its economic policy.

## Incentives compared to Government Grants

The incentive effect of the tax system, as mentioned above, should be clearly distinguished in your mind from Government Grants.

There are many cases such as Regional Development Grants where Government encourages an economic decision in favour of locating a business in a certain area. Where the Government actually pays the business a sum of money, those payments are grants.

Incentives that work through the tax system operate by way of reducing the tax bill if a certain course of action is taken. An example is capital allowances which are intended to encourage business to replace old machinery by allowing a deduction of the cost for tax purposes quicker than would be taken in the accounts of the business.

Incentives of this sort can either produce a reduction or repayment of tax, or they may just allow a delay in payment of tax. However, to obtain any repayment of tax from the Government, the taxpayer (individual or business) must itself have previously paid the tax. That is the main difference between tax incentives and Government grants. You may never have paid any tax yet your business could be eligible to receive certain Government grants.

## Types of Tax

You can take the view that almost any payment to the Government, local authority, or even Nationalised Industries is a form of taxation. We think the Nationalised Industries can be excluded since they are usually providing a service for an economic charge. The present Government expects them to be run on a commercial basis although, in certain cases, the consumer has little choice but to use these services.

There are certain services provided more directly by Government and for which fees are charged. Some, such as fees charged for patent applications or by the Registrar of Companies, can be related to the costs of the relevant Government Department providing the service. These are not taxes if the fee is a reasonable reflection of the cost of providing the service.

Other cases such as Road Tax and National Insurance contributions must be considered to be forms of taxation since changes in amounts charged are based on Government decisions unrelated to the cost of providing the roads or pensions and benefits involved.

Perhaps the best definition of what is or is not taxation is to include as tax any item of Government or Local Authority income which is controlled by Finance Acts passed through Parliament. We would therefore view the following as the main types of tax which can have an impact on the small business:

1. Income Tax including the P.A.Y.E. system (Pay as you Earn).
2. Corporation Tax.
3. Value Added Tax.
4. Capital Gains Tax.
5. Capital Transfer Tax.
6. National Insurance contributions.
7. Local Authority Rates.
8. Stamp Duty and Capital Duty.

## *Your business relationship with the Government*

Whether you are a sole proprietor or own 100% of the shares of a company you should understand that you have a partner. That partner is the Government, and the partnership agreement is the tax system. This seems to us to be the most constructive and positive way to look on this arrangement and we shall now expand on this idea.

Looking on the Government as an enemy attacking you and your business through the tax system is a negative approach. You can be sure of one thing, that attitude will not make them go away. It does not even help to think of it as a 'protection-racket' although that analogy may seem attractive to some people.

Consider yourself fortunate that the Government takes the role of a sleeping partner in your business rather than that of an active equity partner. They tend to dictate the terms of the partnership since it would be chaotic and unfair if, through their agents (Revenue and Customs and Excise) they entered into special deals with each separate business. Such compromises do happen to a limited extent, and when they do they usually produce results which could be considered unfair by the average taxpayer.

So, think positive. You run or want to run a business based in the United Kingdom. Then the Government is a sleeping partner and you should learn as much as you can about your partnership agreement. The rules of the game are to be found in the rules of the tax system. Don't complain about your sleeping partner getting an unfair advantage if you have not bothered to learn the rules of the partnership.

## The 'Partnership' arrangement.

1. The Government is entitled to a share in the profits of your business through taxes.
   This is not a fixed share. It can be varied depending on whether you choose to distribute your profits out of the business. Also it can be reduced if you decide to re-invest your profits in the business or in some new business venture.
2. The Government encourages you in setting up or expanding your business.
3. The Government wants to maximise its Revenue. Taking too large a share of profits will discourage the businessman. It is therefore in the interests of the 'sleeping partner' that the business should prosper and grow. You therefore have a common objective. You are usually free to choose the entity through which you will run the business (yourself, a partnership with others, a co-operative or a limited company).
   There are several ways in which you can get tax relief in raising capital for the business. One example is relief for loan interest paid. In this way, if you have some non-business income subject to tax you can obtain tax relief on loan interest. This may be available where the loan is raised for the purpose of investment in the business activity.
   In some cases the Government helps you to obtain finance from others. The Business Expansion Scheme is an example where the Government gives tax relief to individual taxpayers who are willing to invest in ordinary shares of new or expanding companies.
4. The Government may be willing to reinvest its share of profits. You may be able to take certain investment decisions in your business to delay or avoid having to pay tax on profits already earned. The situations where this can be done are set out in the rules of the tax system. If you invest in new plant or machinery or increase your borrowings to fund expansion the Goverment would usually encourage that. The encouragement is given through tax relief. If you plan well and predict your tax liabilities accurately in line with your other forecasts then you can always measure the true (after tax) cost of any investment decision.
   Whether these incentive effects actually apply will depend on your own business circumstances. If your business has large accumulated tax losses the system will not be offering you a saving in terms of tax payments which you will not be making

in any case. The tax system cannot be flexible enough to be fair or effective in every individual case. It is more important that there is certainty in the tax laws and in their administration. Then, at least, businessmen can plan and make decisions in a relatively stable environment so that the tax effects they expect are actually the tax results they meet.

A point which underlines the sleeping partnership aspect of taxation relates to levels of tax. In the last ten years in the United Kingdom we have seen a distinct change in the levels of taxation. The Conservative Government since 1979 has dramatically reduced the very high rates of income tax, and Capital Transfer Tax. They have made reductions in the rate of Corporation Tax while also reducing the very high first year Capital Allowances. Unfortunately many people have been slow to appreciate the effect of these changes. Therefore the incentive effect to encourage small businesses has been slow to get off the ground.

The previously very high tax rates had a disincentive effect discouraging those with capital from setting-up new businesses. In many cases it actually drove people abroad. The system now favours small business and, apart from the administrative burdens, the tax system is playing its part in encouraging enterprise.

Everyone has a certain sense of fairness which they expect from the tax system. Some situations can arise which seem quite unfair. For example, unlike PAYE a business does not pay most of its tax on a monthly basis in line with its earnings. Therefore tax can often be due for payment a considerable time after the profits are made. If the payment date should happen to be at a time when the business is doing badly it can seem quite unfair that the 'sleeping partner' should be taking its share of old profits at such a time. However, before feeling persecuted the businessman should ask himself whether he has really done enough to understand the tax system and whether he should not have been able (or been advised) to expect the relevant amount of tax as a predictable expense at that time.

The later Chapters of this book should improve your awareness of the tax system and your ability to anticipate (directly or through your advisers) the full tax implications of your business decisions.

## 2. The Starting Point — your personal tax position must be considered always as the background to the taxation of the business

Your personal tax position is obviously in your mind as part of your personal cashflow projections when you plan to start a business. Some people ignore it even then or act on some vague assumption that just by starting a business their personal tax position will improve.

We discuss in a later chapter in detail the question of the tax implications of the choice of business entity. Whatever entity is selected, partnership or company, that question cannot be decided without understanding your own tax position.

You should take the following steps to review your present and future tax position. This process is not just relevant to the business start-up situation. It should be a review you carry out at least once each tax year.

1. The first step is to have your Tax Returns up-to-date and agreed to know your present Income Tax and Capital Gains Tax position.
2. Review your investments and their tax treatment. Could the return (net of tax) from these investments be improved?
3. Review your liabilities such as your mortgage or other loans to see if they are still tax efficient.
4. Review your pension position. Have you made sufficient provision and is it in the most efficient vehicle. Have you fully used your tax relief for pension provision.
5. Consider your family and dependants. In particular review life insurance provision and the likely Capital Transfer Tax burden if you were to die. Have you taken sufficient steps to mitigate the effect of Capital Transfer Tax?

Once you know your own tax position you can then properly assess the personal financial effect of your decisions concerning your business. Given your age and your particular domestic circumstances you can decide your financial objectives.

A young single man may have no interest in the provision of life insurance, pensions or Capital Transfer Tax planning. By comparison, a redundant 55 year old executive from a large company may already be in receipt of an adequate pension. He may want to run his own business to keep active but yet he may wish the benefit of any capital growth in the new business to accrue directly to the benefit of his children.

From reflecting on your own situation in the form of the reviews suggested above it should have become clear that there can be an infinite variety of combinations of personal circumstances. The first point is for you and your advisers to understand your personal situation and financial objectives. Decisions concerning the structure, financing, ownership and growth of the business can then be taken in the proper context to suit your present position and your future aims.

Whether you have the capital to start the business or whether you need to borrow is a significant distinction. In some cases it is important whether you can even earn enough to use your personal Income Tax allowance in a particular tax year.

We shall now look at each of the points listed above in more detail and outline the possible implications these personal tax matters could have for your business.


**Have your Income Tax and Capital Gains Tax position as far up-to-date as possible**

The time of year when you start your business may not be within your control but it could have a significant effect on the level of your own Income Tax and the times at which such tax may be payable. Depending on the type of business you are starting you may be able to time the start so that you have a trading tax loss in the first tax year which might allow you to receive a repayment of tax previously suffered under the PAYE system. (See the section on starting a business in Chapter 8.) That repayment may have the effect of reducing your highest rate of tax (e.g. from 60% to 30%). It might have the adverse effect in some cases of producing a situation where you pay no tax for the year but have not used all your allowances. That would be a poor result if in the following year your profits were high enough to result in tax being payable. Will you continue to have earned income from sources other than the business? In that case you may need to predict that income to calculate properly the tax position of the business. An example would be someone who is say 58 and is receiving a pension from a previous employer as well as running his own business.

Your personal Income Tax position could affect the method you select to finance your business. If you have other income from outside the business then it may be that you can get tax relief on loan interest despite the fact that the business itself is not immediately profitable. The personal tax position of your husband or wife is also relevant. Tax relief may be available to the other party to the marriage against their income although the relief would be of no present value to yourself directly.

**Review your investments and their tax treatment.**

You may have funds invested to meet other long-term aims or just as a safety-net for a rainy day. However you ought to consider carefully, if there is no other over-riding reason, whether you should use those funds for the new business or whether it is more effective from a tax point of view to borrow elsewhere and leave those investments intact.

**Review your liabilities such as your mortgage or other loans to see if they are still tax efficient**

You may already have some borrowings for which you do not obtain tax relief yet you plan to put cash into your business as initial capital. You should consider repaying those loans with the cash available and borrowing afresh to fund the business.

On the other hand you might see from your projections of income in the early years of the business that you are unlikely to get full advantage of your mortgage interest relief. Again a restructuring of your borrowing, replacing the mortgage with a business loan might enable you to carry forward the advantage of the loan interest relief for tax purposes as part of a trading loss. Otherwise the interest payments might never obtain any effective tax relief.

**Review your pension provisions. Have you made sufficient provision and is it in the most efficient vehicle? Have you fully used your tax relief for pension provision?**

It is well known now that a large part of an individual's wealth and future income may be tied up in his pension scheme or schemes. To ignore this aspect of your personal financial position would be a significant omission. The tax system provides numerous incentives to encourage people to make their own provisions for pensions.

These incentives are not restricted to the self-employed but also apply to employees who are not participants in or who do not fully contribute to any company pension scheme.

Increased mobility of labour means that long service with a company is now becoming the exception rather than the rule. Therefore the Government is considering legislation to improve the rights of individuals to transfer their pension provisions when they change jobs. You will no doubt have read or heard recently the phrase 'portable pensions'.

At present it is not clear how far the new rules may go. Also there are doubts about the tax treatment of pension funds and pension contributions remaining stable. Pensions are therefore in a state of flux and some uncertainty from a planning point of view. However, many advantageous aspects exist and any businessman when considering funding the business or what to do to shelter profits from tax should always consider pensions. There is already a lot of portability available and 'loan-back' schemes abound.

Don't look on pension provision as a necessary evil as many do with life assurance. In that way you will end up doing too little too late. Be positive and look on your pension planning as a basic part of your personal and business financial planning. Select the form of pension provision that can provide your business with the greatest flexibility. Above all, each year ask yourself how you justify delay and why you have not considered in detail the after- tax effect of making provision for your pension.

**Example**

Executive (M) aged 45 leaving large company to start his own business. Short of capital for the business and doubtful whether to use the medium of sole trader or a limited company. He had considered the implications of these two types of entity and they appear evenly-matched. However he had not considered any pension implications.

In this case M had the choice on leaving his existing employer to leave his pension and collect a pension from that company at age 60 or to transfer his and the company's pension contributions to another pension scheme. He had 12 months after leaving the company to make his choice. If he decides to use a limited company for his new business he could establish a pension fund for that new company. If it was a proper self-administered fund M could then elect to have his previous pension 'fund' transferred to this new fund. 50% of the assets in this new fund would then be available to lend to M's new company as working capital.

**Consider your family and dependents. In particular review life insurance provision and the likely Capital Transfer Tax burden if you were to die. Have you taken sufficient steps to mitigate the effects of Capital Transfer Tax?**

This may not seem an important matter when you are just starting a new business. It might seem to be more appropriate at a stage when you have built a successful business and when the value of that actual business may be the major asset likely to produce a large Capital Transfer Tax bill on your death.

However, this subject may be of obvious importance to an already wealthy person starting a business. An older person who does not require a large income from the new business but can foresee possibilities, if successful, of significant capital growth, should also consider this question. In the early stages of a new business its value is likely to be low and that may therefore be the best time at which to transfer shares in the business to friends or relations. This is obviously a very personal decision but, if the long term aim is to leave your capital to certain individuals in some cases there is no point waiting. The main factor against such a move may well be your desire to retain control of your business.

Look at your position. You may not even be able to face preparing a will or deciding who you wish to benefit on your death. But if you do have some idea of the way you would like to see your assets distributed you should consider the ownership of your new business. Before it is worth very much at all why not consider giving shares in the new business to those you wish to benefit under your will.

We hope this chapter has underlined the need to assess and understand your personal financial and tax position before approaching setting-up a business. We would also stress that this type of review should be done by yourself at least once a year once the business is in place. There is little point assessing the tax implications of the business forecasts and decisions if any apparent business tax benefits are negated by their effects on your personal position. Try to understand both and then you will be alert to points where they interact.

Partners in a partnership or fellow directors in a small company will often be faced with decisions which benefit the business but may also affect their personal tax position. If you are to be involved in such decisions make sure you are well informed of your personal position.

## 3. The Government representatives and how to deal with them.

The words Inland Revenue or Customs and Excise create strange images in some people's minds. We have met individuals who have accumulated envelopes sent by these bodies and have been too scared even to open them. In one case we found in a bundle of such envelopes one marked 'O.H.M.S.' like the rest but it contained a letter inviting the individual for a job interview with another Goverment Department. Unfortunately the date of the interview had passed!

As we have already said it is the Government that makes the tax laws and it is the Government that takes the benefit of the taxes paid. These other bodies or groups of individuals are just the agents employed by the Government to administer the tax laws, to check and agree tax liabilities in accordance with those laws and to enforce the allocation of such agreed tax liabilities. Debt collectors are never very popular but if you anticipate the debt you should provide for it. If you consider that you are being treated unreasonably or unfairly by these Government agents then there are adequate means through which to voice such complaints.

It is important to view Civil Service Departments in terms of the individuals within them and in particular the individuals dealing with your tax affairs or those of your business. These individuals are usually approachable and reasonable. They have a job to do and you might as well co-operate and help them in achieving their assigned objectives. These individuals cannot change the tax law however unfair a particular aspect of it may seem to you. In some situations these individual civil servants do have some discretionary powers but you are more likely to benefit from any such discretion if you are being helpful and constructive in relation to your tax affairs.

As was mentioned in the first book in this series, *Starting a Small Business*

'the best way to bear the bureaucrats . . . is to join them . . .

13

Bureaucrats are human beings – admittedly some more so than others – but all are definitely human.

Seriously though, such people as the Inspector of Taxes, the VAT man, the D.H.S.S. and so on are becoming more helpful and increasingly aware of their need to aid the small businessman.'

We would endorse that view and encourage you not to be afraid to approach these departments yourself and seek their advice. The Revenue issue a series of particularly good leaflets explaining in detail certain aspects of the tax system. These are as good, if not better than, any tax guides issued outside the Revenue and are very reliable sources of information. A list of these publications is given in Appendix I. They are free on request at any of the Revenue Offices. Get hold of any you think cover topics relevant to yourself and if you don't understand any part of them visit the enquiry desk at your local Inspector of Taxes office and ask them to explain in more detail.

## The Inland Revenue

One basic source of misunderstanding results from the fact that the Revenue is divided into two distinct parts. Any individual taxpayer in business will have to deal with both parts of the Inland Revenue and it cannot be assumed that communications between them are very good. The two parts you will have to deal with are the Inspector of Taxes and the Collector of Taxes.

The Inspector's office deals with your Tax Returns and accounts and decides (subject to any appeals) how much tax you have to pay for a particular tax year. The Inspector then advises the Collector of the amount of tax due and the Collector's office takes over and issues demands for payment.

The Collector can therefore be seen as a form of debt collector. He will use all the powers available to him to collect the money due and any penalties for late payment. The important point to note from all this is that the Collector has no power to alter the figure of tax payable. The Collector has no knowledge of any discussions between you and the Inspector regarding the amount for which you are liable.

What often happens, therefore, is that the information flowing from the Inspector to the Collector may be delayed or incorrect. In such circumstances you could therefoe receive a personal visit to your office or home from a representative of the Collector's office.

14

In such a case people are often indignant that the visitor does not know the background or details of recent correspondence between the taxpayer and the Inspector.

## The Collector of Taxes

The role of the Collector of Taxes is therefore a simple one to understand. He acts as an official debt collector for the Revenue. His office does not issue assessments to tax. However, based on assessments issued by the Inspector of Taxes, the Collector then issues demand notices to the taxpayer as the first approach to collect the amount of tax assessed.

If the taxpayer enters an appeal against a tax assessment then, the tax subject to appeal should not be demanded by the Collector pending the outcome of the appeal hearing or pending earlier agreement between the Inspector of Taxes and the taxpayer.

You will appreciate therefore the administration involved when you submit such an appeal against an assessment. On receipt of your appeal the Inspector's office should notify the Collector as to any alteration of the amount of tax then due on the assessment subject to the appeal. If there is any delay in this notification, then the Collector will continue to collect tax claimed under the original assessment. To get the position rectified you need to contact the Inspector who will in turn contact the Collector. You must remember the Collector cannot act without the Inspector's authority.

## The Inspector of Taxes

The role of the office of Inspector of Taxes is to ascertain the facts relevant to the income of a taxpayer and then to apply the tax law and Revenue practice to decide the amount of tax payable. Whatever decisions the Inspector takes can be the subject of an appeal by the taxpayer. The right of appeal lies first to the General Commissioners of Tax. If dissatisfied however, the taxpayer, or the Revenue have the right to appeal again to the High Court.

Any individual taxpayer has the choice of whether to deal directly with the Inspector of Taxes or to appoint an agent such as an accountant to so act. Whoever the agent may be the legislation means that the Revenue refer to the agent as a 'tax accountant' which tends to perpetuate the myth that you need to have an accountant dealing with your tax affairs. The question of the use of advisers is dealt with in a later Chapter. For the present it is enough to say that we recommend that you try to understand the tax system and how the Revenue operate even if you do use an agent to represent your case to the Revenue.

To appoint an agent to act on your behalf in dealing with the Revenue you need to sign a Revenue Form 64-8. This form authorises the Revenue to talk to the agent. You will receive original assessments and the agent should receive a copy. However you will not be sent any other correspondence or any amendments to assessments. If you no longer wish to use an agent or wish to use another person then you must complete another Form 64-8, sign it and send it to the Inspector of Taxes dealing with your tax affairs.

## H.M. Customs & Excise

You will only have to deal with this arm of the Government if your business has sufficient turnover to have to register for the purposes of Value Added Tax (VAT) or, in the unlikely circumstances that you are below the registration levels but purport to charge VAT to customers. (Details about VAT Registration are given in Appendix VII).

H.M. Customs and Excise, in dealing with VAT, is not divided in the way that the Inland Revenue divides the functions of Inspector and Collector. V.A.T. being a relatively recent introduction to the tax system is controlled within H.M. Customs and Excise by a single central office and computer system. This makes this department more efficient than the Inland Revenue in terms of the timely issue of Returns. The system is also rigid in relation to payment or repayment of the tax.

Local offices of H.M. Customs and Excise do however get involved and if you are registered for VAT you are almost bound to be visited by a representative of the local office within a short time of starting to trade. The purpose of such visits is to ensure that your book-keeping and accounting systems and records are adequate and that those books record the transactions of the business in order to enable you to prepare reliable VAT Returns. The visit will also involve an extremely detailed review of actual transactions to date.

That is a reasonable objective if the visit is used to consider the general VAT treatment of the normal significant transactions of the business. However, in our experience the amount of detailed work done by H.M. Customs and Excise representatives on such visits seems excessive and often of questionable value in terms of collectable VAT raised when compared with the time spent.

The important points to realise are that:

1. You have not been singled-out for some type of special investigation;
2. You should ensure that your books of account are set-up properly and kept up-to-date to a standard sufficient for VAT purposes;
3. You should expect further visits on future occasions if there is any marked variation in the pattern of your trading.

This last point stems from the centralised computer systems which were established for VAT. This enables the Customs and Excise officials to work on the basis of exception reports produced by the computer. Thus a local office can receive each month a list of businesses in their area which deserve a visit. That list would include a business for which VAT Returns had not been received or a business for which the Returns show an unusual trend of activity compared with previous Returns. The computer also enables a comparison to be drawn between the Returns of different businesses in the same industry.

As with the Inland Revenue the local VAT offices can provide you with advice if you are doubtful on the VAT treatment of a particular transaction. They also provide detailed leaflets explaining different aspects of VAT.

In the 1985 Budget the Chancellor announced that the recommendations of the Keith Committee with regard to the collection of VAT were to be implimented. This means that collection procedures will be tightened up as follows:-

(i) There will be interest penalties on late payment.
(ii) There will be default surcharges where the VAT return is submitted late on more than two successive occasions in two years.
(iii) Where the return understates the liability by more than a certain percentage, there will be penalties of 30% of the amount understated.
(iv) Records will have to be kept for six years instead of three.
(v) There are tougher criminal penalties for fraud, the maximum sentence being increased from two years to seven.

# 4. The Administrative Aspects of Tax

In this chapter we shall deal with administration of tax in two parts. The first is the administrative system of the Revenue and the second is the administration of your business to fit in with the tax system.

## The Revenue's administrative system

Whether you are dealing with Income Tax, or Corporation Tax the basic structure of the tax administrative system is very similar.

### Administration

The statutory provisions dealing with the administration of Income Tax are found within the Taxes Management Act 1970.

The administration is carried out by the Board of Inland Revenue, and for this purpose the U.K. is divided into a number of regions each headed by a Regional Controller. The Regional Controller in turn is in charge of the Inspectors of Taxes and Collectors of Taxes who are assigned to the various Tax Districts within each region.

It is an essential part of the administration that the collection of tax and assessment of tax are dealt with entirely separately. You will normally not deal directly with the Collector of Taxes, except to pay tax; all your negotiation being with the Inspector of Taxes in the District in which your affairs are handled.

Once the procedure for collection of tax is in the hands of the Collector it will not be stopped until the Inspector informs the Collector that collection is no longer due. It is thus essential not to wait for demand notes before dealing with your tax affairs because by that time all scope for negotiation will most likely have been lost.

## Inspector of Taxes

The duties of the Inspector are:
(a) The issue of Tax Returns.
(b) Review of Tax Returns.
(c) Issue of tax assessments based on Tax Returns and on any other additional information obtained.
(d) Issue of estimated tax assessments where no Tax Return is received or where the Inspector disagrees with its contents.
(e) Administration of appeals made by the taxpayer and, where possible, settlement of appeals by agreement.
(f) Listing of appeals for hearing before the Commissioners of Income Tax where settlement by agreement is not possible, and appearing before the Commissioners to put the Revenue's case (the Commissioners act as a local tax court of first instance).
(g) Issue of PAYE codes and supervision of employees' returns.

## Tax Districts

The Tax District which deals with your tax affairs is not necessarily where you live. If you are employed it will be the District where your employer is based, and in the case of centralised payroll systems where your employer's head office is located. Owing to government decentralisation policy many of the London PAYE Districts are in Wales and Scotland. If you are self-employed the Tax District dealing with the tax affairs of that business will be the District in which the business is based.

It is possible to have a number of Districts dealing with your tax affairs simultaneously. For example in the case of husband and wife who are both employees and are also self-employed, there could be four Districts involved. One each for the employment earnings, and one each for the self-employed earnings.

If you are an employee as well as having self-employed earnings, the District dealing with your business will usually agree the profits/losses of the business independently. They then advise the District dealing with the other earnings, (the District from which the Tax Return was issued), of those profits/losses.

Confusion may arise where more than one District is handling your tax affairs. To assist in handling these problems the Government has recently set up local enquiry offices where the public can go with specific problems to get over-the-counter help rather than having to phone a District based in another part of the country. If using your local telephone directory to find your local enquiry office, look under Inland Revenue, *not* Tax Office. (especially if you live in Woking our business gets several calls a day asking for the tax office!)

## Collection of Tax

Tax is deducted by two means:
(a) by deduction at source;
(b) by direct assessment.

## Self-Employed

If you are self-employed the majority of your tax is collected by DIRECT ASSESSMENT, some time after you have actually earned the income. Your communication with the Collector of Taxes should only be in relation to the payment of tax assessed by the Inspector.

## Tax Returns

In law you are required to make Returns of income for the purpose of tax. The frequency with which such Returns is required varies, but is usually annual. In practice these Returns are usually issued by the Revenue authorities to the individual (or company) taxpayer.

Once the Return is received the Inspector of Taxes may write to the taxpayer or his agent requesting further disclosure or clarification of certain items relating to the Return period. Some of these questions may be prompted by information about the taxpayer, that the Inspector has gained from other sources. Such sources could include newspaper articles or other Inspectors of Taxes who deal with other taxpayers with whom your business may have traded during that period. Inspectors of Taxes have many ways of finding out about individuals, and apparently one of the most common sources is informants. Don't exaggerate and boast about things to your friends in the pub or it could lead to a lot of unnecessary trouble for yourself and the Revenue.

## Assessments to tax

In the absence of a Return or if the Return provides insufficient information the Inspector will raise an estimated assessment. In preparing this document the Inspector will use an estimated figure of income. The purpose of issuing such an assessment is to put pressure on the taxpayer or his agent to provide the correct information.

An estimated assessment has this effect because its issue starts a process leading to the collection of the tax assessed. In order to stop that process the taxpayer has to appeal against the assessment within 30 days. In the case of most assessments the taxpayer has to provide an estimate of the true liability. If the taxpayer's estimate later proves too low then he may suffer penalties of high interest payable to the Revenue.

Even when the Inspector has the Return and all necessary information in good time it is necessary for him to raise an assessment to tax in order to start the process of collecting the tax due. It is still possible for you to appeal against an assessment based on actual figures of income and allowances if you believe it does not show your proper tax liability.

An estimated assessment is distinguished by the use of a letter 'E' beside the figure of income or profit assessed. Even if an assessment is not estimated in that distinctive way it may be wrong. It could be a typing error or just that the Inspector has assessed a figure shown in this year's Return when he should have assessed a figure shown in last year's Return.

If no appeal is entered within the 30 day limit then an assessment (even an estimated one) becomes final and the collection process takes over. In rare cases an Inspector may allow a late appeal but don't depend on that.

## Appeals

The Revenue issue special pink forms with assessments. These forms are the ones you use to enter an appeal and to apply for postponement of any tax you consider to be in excess of your proper liability. You could just appeal by way of a letter to the Inspector. However, the Revenue especially ask taxpayers to use the pink appeal forms. When the post is opened in the Inspector's office special priority is given to processing these pink appeal forms.

If the receipt of an appeal, against a particular assessment, has not been processed within the 30 day limit the Inspector will not have notified the Collector of Taxes office of the appeal and therefore the demands from the Collector for the tax will increase. It is in your interest to make any appeal against an assessment as promptly as possible and to use the Revenue's pink form to enter the appeal.

An appeal against an assessment to tax can be made to either the General or the Special Commissioners of Income Tax. Such appeals are usually made to the General Commissioners. When you make an appeal you should always make clear the assessment you are appealing against and your groundsof appeal. If you do not use the Revenue form you should always quote:

Date of Assessment;
Assessment Number;
Type of Assessment;
Tax Assessed;
Grounds of Appeal.

At the same time as entering an appeal you may apply to postpone the payment of some or all of the tax charged on the assessment. In the case of the appeal and the postponement application you have to give your reasons. Postponement of tax is advisable where you are sure that the tax assessed is more than your liability. If you are not sure you must be careful since you could run into interest penalties if you get it wrong. Postponement of tax is not available as a right. You make the application and if the Inspector is satisfied with the reasons you give he will then reply agreeing to the postponement of tax.

You may receive from the Inspector a revised assessment, being a revision of an earlier one for the same tax year. Assuming you have already entered an appeal against the first assessment there is no need to appeal against the revised assessment. If you still disagree with the amounts in the revised assessment you should advise the Inspector by letter.

**Collection of Tax**

Once an assessment has been issued the Collector takes on the responsibility of chasing you for the payment of the tax due. He cannot enter into negotiations about your liability. That is a question only for the Inspector. Assessments usually state on them the due date for payment and include payslips showing the amount payable together with notes explaining methods of payment.

If payment is not made when due the Collector will issue demand notes for the tax. If non-payment continues you will receive a final demand. The next step is for the normal court proceedings to be started as for any debt. This is usually preceded by a personal visit by one of the Collector's staff to your business premises as a final effort to avoid the court proceedings.

The process outlined above can only be stopped completely if the assessment is vacated or finally agreed by the Inspector at a level equal to or below the amount of tax already paid by you. The process can be delayed but not actually stopped for good by you entering an appeal.

In either case the Collector acts only on instructions from the Inspector. Sometimes such instructions are delayed and there are frequent cases of the collection process continuing despite the taxpayer or his agent having previously agreed the proper liability with the Inspector. Your course of action in these circumstances should be first to contact the Inspector. He will then contact the Collector.

If a repayment of tax is due to you that will be paid by the Collector of Taxes again acting on the instruction of the Inspector.

## Interest Penalties

Interest on overdue tax may be payable usually running from the date the tax is payable or 30 days from the issue of the assessment whichever is the later date. It is intended to act as a penalty. It is currently 11% but it should be noted that the interest is not itself allowed as a deduction for tax purposes.

On the other hand, you can sometimes qualify for a tax-free interest payment from the Revenue. This can happen if tax has been overpaid and the repayment is more than one year after the end of the year of assessment. This is called repayment supplement and is also 11%.

## *Your own business administration*

The need to keep proper accounting records for your business has been made clear in other books in this series. The major requirement is to be able to budget for and control your income and expenditure. Since tax could be one of the major forms of your business expenditure what we have to say here just underlines the need to keep good records and to plan ahead.

If you are dealing with the tax affairs of your business yourself then you need to set up procedures to anticipate dates when tax payments will be due. You should also include the tax effects in any forward planning and then see whether the tax anticipated to be due could be reduced by taking a different course of action.

If your business tax affairs are dealt with by an accountant or other person you must ensure a smooth and prompt flow of information so that you have as much warning as possible as to the amount and timing of tax payments. We shall discuss in detail in the next Chapter the problems of dealing with the Revenue through an accountant or other agent.

# 5. The structure of the tax system

*Finance Acts and changes in Tax Law*

As mentioned in Chapter I, the laws and structure of the tax system are laid down in the Taxes Acts.

Each year and sometimes more frequently, a Finance Act is passed through Parliament. This Act will contain both amending legislation which amends previous Acts, and new legislation. If you have not been trained to read the legislation it can be confusing finding your way around the different Acts. If you are using a tax adviser in relation to some difficult point, try and ensure that he is reading the legislation and not relying entirely on a textbook which may not be correct. Ask him in his advice to set out references to the legislation which apply to your problem.

The main Finance Act each year originates from the Chancellor's Budget Speech which is given sometime in March. Two to three weeks after that speech, a Finance Bill is published which gives draft legislation covering all announcements made in the Budget. This Bill is debated in Parliament both in committee stage and on the floor of the House.

When all relevant changes have been made it passes to the House of Lords, and then finally receives the Royal Assent, being published as the Finance Act of the year e.g. Finance Act 1985 will receive the Royal Assent sometime in July or August 1985. Amendments may well have been made so that the Finance Act which becomes law may be different from the Budget speech proposals.

The rates of Income Tax and personal allowances for each tax year are announced in March in the Budget for the following tax year. For example, the March 85 Budget announced allowances and rates for the tax year 1985/86 – 6th April, 1985 to 5th April, 1986. The rates may change during the passage of the bill through Parliament, but they usually do not. Corporation Tax rates are normally fixed in arrears. The March 85 Budget fixed the rate for the year to 31st March, 1985. However, the rate had not changed much in the years up to March, 1984 when the Chancellor announced a reduction in rates spreading some way into the future. This is of great assistance to businesses in tax planning and helps in creating an air of stability.

## Different types of income have different tax rates

We assume that all individuals reading this book because they have a business in the UK are RESIDENT and ORDINARILY RESIDENT in the U.K. for tax purposes. In outline, you are regarded as Resident in the U.K. if you are physically present here for 183 days in the tax year, and Ordinarily Resident here if you are habitually Resident here year after year. It is usually very difficult to run a business in the U.K. without being regarded as Resident in the U.K.

## Sources of Income

A U.K. RESIDENT and ORDINARILY RESIDENT individual is charged to income tax on all sources of income wherever they arise. Technically, the income is divided into a number of sources or classes and different rules apply to the different classes. These are listed below:

## Classes of Income

### Schedule A

Income from land and buildings including rents and certain premiums from leases.

### Schedule B

The 'assessable value' of woodlands that are managed on a commercial basis.

## Schedule C

Income from 'gilt-edged securities' payable in the United Kingdom as well as certain overseas public revenue dividends that are paid through a banker or other person in the U.K. (paying agent). The tax is assessed on the paying agent, rather than on the recipient.

## Schedule D

This is divided into the following separate 'Cases':

| | |
|---|---|
| Case I | Trades |
| Case II | Professions or vocations |
| Case III | Interest received, annuities and other annual payments |
| Case IV & V | Overseas income from certain investments, possessions and businesses |
| Case VI | Miscellaneous profits not falling within any of the other Cases of Schedule D. |

## Schedule E

Wages and salaries from employments (including directorships). There are the following 'Cases':

| | |
|---|---|
| Case I | Taxpayer is RESIDENT and ORDINARILY RESIDENT in the U.K. except for 'foreign emoluments.' |
| Case II | Taxpayer is NON-RESIDENT or RESIDENT, but *not* ORDINARILY RESIDENT, except for 'foreign emoluments'. |
| Case III | Taxpayer is RESIDENT, but not ORDINARILY RESIDENT and emoluments are for work performed wholly or partly overseas and 'foreign emoluments' where taxpayer is RESIDENT and ORDINARILY RESIDENT and the work is performed wholly overseas. |

## Schedule F

Dividends paid by companies and certain other distributions that they make.

To be able to find out which tax rules apply to a particular part of your income you first need to find out which Schedule or Case the income is taxed under and then look up the rules applicable to that income.

Most of the tax rules in this book relate to Schedule D Cases I and II and Schedule E, because these are the main schedules affecting a business. However you might also have property income and interest income included in your business profits. These sources of income must be separated out and taxed under Schedule A and Schedule D Case III respectively.

This system of Cases and Schedules may seem meaningless at first sight, but they are very important when it comes to using losses and claiming allowances which may be restricted to being relieved against income from one particular case or Schedule.

## Domicile

We have mentioned above the relevance for tax purposes of your UK residence status. Domicile is another important aspect of your status which must be considered and which can have a significant influence on an individual's tax position.

### Determination of domicile under U.K. law

Unlike residence it is only possible to be domiciled in one country at a time. As a general rule a person is domiciled in the country in which he has his permanent home. Every person acquires a domicile of origin at birth (normally this will follow the domicile of his father) and every person with the necessary legal capacity (in the U.K. he must be over 16) can change this domicile.

To acquire this new domicile, or the domicile of choice as it is called, two stringent tests must be satisfied. The first is that the person must be resident in the new country and the second requires the intention of the party to stay in that country indefinitely – and these two must coincide.

In deciding whether a domicile of choice has been acquired the English Courts will look at the actual circumstances both past and potential. In order to prove an intention to stay in the new country permanently the acquisition of a new permanent home is very important as is the ending of most contacts with the domicile of origin. Thus in practical terms for a foreign national to acquire a domicile in the U.K. he must effectively set up a new home in the U.K. and abandon any thoughts of returning to his original country.

# 6. Outside help

One of the basic decisions you must make when contemplating setting up your business is whether you need outside advice in relation to tax. For such a complex subject it is advisable to seek some outside advice. However, we would advise you not to abdicate responsibility for tax to such an adviser. You may make him your agent in dealing with the Revenue but don't then take the view that you cannot understand tax and leave it entirely in his hands.

Obviously some taxpayers, even some in business on their own account, cannot understand much about their own tax affairs. However, if you are capable of understanding you should make the effort to do so. Knowledge of the tax effects of your business decisions will make you a better manager of your business. Don't let the tax aspects take contol but try to understand them and put them in the balance in proportion to the other facts to be considered in reaching a decision.

*Where to go for advice.*

Most people select a tax adviser on the basis of reputation or recommendation. Traditionally in the United Kingdom accountants have been the usual source of tax advice. This is in contrast to many other countries where tax work has often been undertaken by lawyers.

In the UK the requirement for companies to have their accounts audited has led to the auditors usually acting also in helping the company prepare and submit its Tax Returns or computations. Lawyers only tend to get involved if a specific point relating to the Tax Return is in dispute with the Revenue and might result in litigation. Lawyers are also consulted on tax planning questions if the accountant is unsure of the interpretation of a particular piece of tax legislation.

There are many types and qualities of accountant. Unlike the description 'solicitor' the label 'accountant' does not guarantee that the individual is qualified or experienced in relation to tax. Most people refer to 'accountants' when talking about tax advice. Even the Taxes Management Act strengthens this bias. In that Act 'tax accountant' is defined for certain purposes as follows; 'a person stands in relation to another as tax accountant at any time when he assists the other in the preparation of Returns or accounts to be made or delivered by the other for any purpose of tax;'

So you should look more widely at possible sources of help on tax matters. No part of the accountancy profession has a monopoly on either the preparation of accounts or the provision of tax services. Other sources can include:

Banks

Members of the Institute of Taxation

Other tax consultants

Retired officers of the Inland Revenue

Trade associations

Letters to the financial press

Their description does not matter what is important is to obtain the right balance between cost and the quality of advice and service. Don't just rely on the fact of a friend's recommendation, before hiring a tax adviser. First question that adviser to ensure he is suitable for your purposes. Second, set down some ground rules for doing business together then, if he does not meet the agreed standards or deadlines you can justifiably complain.

## Suitability for your business

Ask your potential tax adviser the following questions:

1. How much does he know about your particular type of business?
2. In his experience does your type of business have particular tax problems and if so has he experience of dealing with these problems?
3. Does he specialise in providing tax services to a business the size of yours?
4. Does he have the time to ensure your business gets a good and prompt service?
5. How does he charge for his work?
6. Can he provide a quotation or at least an estimate for the cost of the work for the first quarter or year (whichever time period is appropriate)?

You are buying a service and you should avoid the attitude some professions give that it is a privilege to be a client. You can only judge after the event whether it has really been a privilege. To start with you must assess the likelihood of the new adviser meeting the standards you require. Like buying a car you want assurance as to quality, reliability, date of delivery and price.

*Establish the standards you expect.*

Market Research we have done shows that most people using tax advisers are satisfied with the quality of service
  (a) because they cannot judge it
  (b) because they have nothing with which to compare it.
You could take the same abject view of a skilled employee. 'He's the best I've got, but he's the only mechanic I employ!' Does that situation stop you setting standards for your staff and judging their performance against such expectations?
We suggest you take the following steps:
1. Ask your new adviser for a summary of the work he expects to have to do during the coming year.
2. Agree a timetable with him as to when your accounts and Tax Return will be ready.
3. Ask him for an estimate of your liability based on your own projections.
4. Ask whether any of that anticipated tax liability could be delayed or avoided and see whether those possible courses of action would fit with your business plans.
After you have set a timetable ensure that you play your part to the full. If you are late in providing him with information then he could use that as an excuse for his own delay. You may be competing for time with many other clients. If you do not express your displeasure at any unjustified delay you may well experience similar delays in the future. Demand prompt service. If he cannot provide it consider taking your business elsewhere.

The second aspect on which you have to judge is the quality of the work. You cannot do this very well unless you learn a bit about the tax system as it applies to your business. Therefore compare the actual tax outcome with that forecast at the start of the year. If it is a lot different consider whether that is explained by any significant difference in your trading position compared with your own forecast. If that does not explain it ask the adviser for his explanation. Don't give up if you cannot understand it. He should be able to communicate with you at a level you can understand. If it still does not make sense perhaps you ought to seek a second opinion or find a tax adviser who can explain your tax affairs to you properly.

Even if you are satisfied don't treat the above approach as being for the first year only and then abandon yourself to doing whatever he tells you in relation to tax. Continue to ask for estimates of liabilities, and any tax planning advice. Continue to agree a timetable adequate for the requirements of your business.

As with all things in your business you need to keep a sense of proportion. Sometimes your adviser may get carried away in lengthy research or correspondence with the Revenue on some technical tax point. That is fine and you don't mind paying his fees if the sum of money involved is significant and when reduced by the chance of success sufficiently outweighs the likely fees. The present value of the tax deduction available is also relevant. If you have large accumulated tax losses for your business adding to those losses may mean the additional loss will not actually save you a cash payment of tax for many years.

The ideal situation is therefore to insist that you be advised as soon as the Revenue raise any question on your accounts or tax computation. Ask for an explanation of what the Inspector might be seeking to attack or disallow. Ask also for an estimate of the likely cost to the business both in the past and for the future and the likelihood of the Revenue conceding.

In other words insist on being informed of progress and express your opinion as to whether a point should be conceded. It is possible to concede for one year stating that you are taking that course in order to settle that year but without prejudice to your right to still argue the same point in a future year. In the future year the same item may have a more significant impact.

Don't dictate too strictly to your adviser. For example, if you say that on no account should excess funds be left in the business you may find that you only receive from him advice consistent with a policy of full distribution. State preferences but don't be too dogmatic or you will receive limited planning advice.

# 7. Tax evasion and tax avoidance

It is important to distinguish between tax evasion and tax avoidance. Evasion of tax involves fraud either in terms of the falsification of accounts or the failure of a taxpayer to disclose a source of income. This is likely to be undertaken by a taxpayer on his own since his adviser would be unlikely (and foolish) to assist him in this course of action.

Tax avoidance, on the other hand, is legal. Within the rules of the system there are many courses of action open to a taxpayer which may enable him to reduce his tax liability. There has been much publicity in recent years about the Revenue and the Courts clamping down on artificial avoidance schemes. From this it might appear that such schemes amounted to evasion rather than avoidance. Clearly there is a grey area between avoidance and evasion. Rather than trying to draw a distinct dividing line it would be best to describe that grey area as artificial avoidance.

The most important point is that we described tax avoidance as action taken 'within the rules of the tax system'. A course of action is likely to be considered artificial tax avoidance if it has no commercial substance and is clearly carried out with the sole purpose of avoiding tax.

## Tax evasion

You hear lots of comments to the effect that, if you have your own business you are able to fiddle your taxes. The normal assumption is that if you are dealing with a lot of cash then you can divert it out of the business and fail to record income. Alternatively people may be tempted to falsify expenditure. You should think very hard before you succumb to such temptations. Apart from the obvious risk of penalties or criminal prosecution tax evasion may harm you in other ways.

If you have made your income artificially low this could punish you if you then want to provide for a pension or if you apply for a mortgage. To obtain a mortgage you may be tempted to give the lender details of your true income and that could be the way you are found out.

You may think as you get older that you have managed to hide funds away and that those funds will be available to your family. However it is quite likely that this situation will come to light on your death and your estate may be greatly diminished as a result.

So, if you indulge in tax evasion you may have many sleepless nights and you will live in fear of being caught. Yet all the time you might have been able to use tax avoidance and planning as a legitimate means of reducing your income tax bill to the same extent.

## *Artificial tax avoidance*

There is not much point entering into complicated schemes and transactions which do not reflect the commercial reality of your business and which are uncertain in their effect. Many taxpayers are still awaiting the outcome of such schemes which were entered into during the 1970's. Such schemes came under Revenue attack and subsequent court decisions have come down against artificial schemes.

These schemes relied on the fact that UK tax law put more emphasis on form than substance. That is to say that individual transactions are considered to be whatever any document or agreement shows them to be. The UK courts did not look behind a transaction or series of transactions to consider the actual effect. In other words they did not look at the substance of the transactions in deciding their effect.

It was assumed that the Revenue could not look through the formality of a series of transactions which would therefore have to be treated as separate transactions. However, the House of Lords decided that, although the substance of a transaction should not take precedence over form the Revenue could look through a series of transactions if it could be shown that the only reason for them to be undertaken was to avoid tax.

Therefore, in any tax planning situation you must review what is being done to ensure that it could not be considered artificial tax avoidance and thus be ineffective.

## Tax avoidance

Taking action within the rules of the tax system to avoid tax can cover a very wide spectrum. Some 'avoidance' is actually encouraged by the Government and Inland Revenue. Other forms of avoidance are discouraged by the introduction of specific anti-avoidance legislation.

The Government tries to frame the tax legislation to produce certain effects to suit its economic and social policy. If that legislation proves ineffective then the Government may act to amend it. Since tax legislation is usually changed only in the annual Finance Act the practice has arisen in recent years for the Chancellor of the Exchequer sometimes to announce a change in advance. Thus he states that a change will be introduced in the following Finance Act but that it will have retrospective effect from the date of his actual announcement.

That is the likely course of action if there is a form of tax avoidance of which the Government does not approve. As the avoidance becomes more widespread it obviously attracts publicity. If it is contrary to Government policy or likely to have a significant detrimental effect on Government Tax Revenue then a particular form of tax avoidance is likely to be stopped.

Examples of tax avoidance encouraged by the Government are as follows;
1. Tax relief under the Business Expansion Scheme.
2. Tax relief for pension premiums.
3. The use of deeds of covenant to pay money to students. This example is even encouraged to the extent that the Revenue publish an explanatory leaflet to help parents prepare such deeds.

In all of these cases, and in others, it is clear that the Government is using the avoidance of tax as an incentive for taxpayers to take action in line with economic policy. The Government at present wants to encourage investment in small companies, the provision of pensions and parental support to students.

Tax avoidance is therefore effective tax planning which is what we are trying to encourage in this book. Take an active interest in your tax affairs and those of your business. Keep your tax affairs up to date and plan your future tax position. Then balance your financial position and plans with a policy of taking the best possible advantage of incentives in the tax system that will enable you to avoid tax. Do not take up schemes where the outcome is uncertain. Go for things which give a definite saving which can be quantified and relied on.

# Trading Entities

This second section of the book deals first with the choice of trading entity and then in some detail with the tax treatment of the main specific types of trading entity. Those types of trading entity are, sole trader, partnership and company.

Although this section of the book goes into some detail it is not intended to be a textbook. Tax textbooks need to be rewritten with every Finance Act. We have tried to cover these topics in a general way that should not require updating except perhaps a little in relation to the Appendices.

We hope this 'trading entities' section will provide you with a reasonable understanding of the tax treatment of the type of business entity you are in. It also gives you a chance to compare that with the tax treatment of alternative types of trading entity. If you have not yet started your business this section should help you to decide which type of trading entity will suit you best.

# 8. Choice of Trading Entity

The choice of trading entity is not necessarily to be determined by the tax benefits or disadvantages of that entity. If this was so then everyone would trade through the same type of organisation. However, the tax differences are significant, and should be borne in mind when making your decision. If tax benefits can blend with your objectives then this is all to the good.

There are three main types of entity:

Sole Trader

Partnership

Company

These three could be reduced to two if you regard partnership and sole trader as the same. They are very similar as regards their taxation but different in other respects and therefore deserve separate consideration.

The detailed rules regarding the taxation of each of these three types of entity is given in chapters 9 to 11 which follow.

The first questions to ask are not necessarily tax related, but having answered those questions, tax will give you a guideline of the direction in which to go.

1. Do you wish to be in business alone or with others?

   If you wish to be alone then a partnership is ruled out. You can always change your mind later.

2. Do you require limited liability?

   People often require limited liability because of the nature of their work. If they were sued as an individual they could be made bankrupt but if their company is sued only the company's assets are lost. For example, an electrician may feel that on large jobs using sub-contractors limited liability is essential. It is possible to insure against being sued for damages, but the cost is often very high which makes a company a cheap form of security. If you do choose a company for this purpose then you should not accumulate profits in the company, they could be lost.

3. What level of profits do you anticipate?

   If you expect to earn profits in the same region as you might reach as an employee, then the cost of a company may be too high. There will be little or no tax saving and you will have to incur the following fees:

   Company Set-up Costs
   Annual Registration Fee
   Annual Audit Fee
   Higher National Insurance Contributions

4. Is pension provision and security of paramount importance?

   If it is, then a company would be preferable. The pension arrangements available in a company are superior to those for self-employed individuals or partners in a partnership. Self-employed people may pay 17.5% of their 'net relevant earnings', (broadly speaking taxable earnings) as Retirement Annuity Premiums to fund a pension. In a company, you may fund as much as is required to give a pension equal to two thirds final salary. If your salary is high, then this percentage can be very large.

   We have had quotes where premiums as much as 45% of salary could be paid into a pension scheme in certain years. The other security available with a company comes with the payment of higher National Insurance contributions in a company. You are entitled to both sickness benefit and unemployment benefit if you lose your job after working for a company. This is not available as a self-employed individual.

5. Do you wish to accumulate wealth?

   This is a difficult question to answer and advise on. It is possible to accumulate wealth both as a sole trader or through a company. However, if the trading profits are very high, then you will be paying most of your tax at 60% as a sole trader compared with say 35% in the company. (see chapter 10). This is a significant difference, and therefore a company is more favourable the higher the expected profits.

   If you and others associated with you control the company then you have what is called a 'close' company and there is a limit to which you can accumulate funds in the company. However, so long as you are trading in the company, and the business is expanding this should not be a problem.

6. Do you need outside help to finance the business?

   It is generally easier to finance a company than a partnership. A financier can take shares and not necessarily interfere with the running of the business. A partner is much more likely to interfere even if he is a 'sleeping partner', or limited partner.

7. Do you wish your family to share in the hoped-for success of the business?

   If you know this at the outset you can give them shares at the start of the business if you form a company. If the business succeeds then you have transferred a substantial portion of your wealth free of CTT. This is not nearly so easy to achieve as a sole trader, even though there is business relief for capital transfer tax.

On balance, we would recommend being a sole trader below £50,000 of profits and thereafter consider a company. There are special tax concessions for transferring the trade of a sole trader to a company, but the reverse process is not so easy. So it may be simpler to start as a sole trader and then incorporate unless you know at the outset that a company is required.

Many individuals who are currently employed by companies and thinking of working as subcontractors to the same employer and similar employers, set up companies to avoid paying PAYE on their earnings from their sub-contract work. If in your own business you are providing services almost exclusively to one customer you ought to take care if you have not selected the use of a limited company as your trading entity.

The Revenue are likely to challenge a situation where you are claiming to be self-employed but are otherwise acting like any other employee. If the Revenue are successful in challenging such a situation then the 'employer' will be forced to apply the normal PAYE rules and to deduct tax and national insurance from the payments made to you.

In judging whether you are an employee or self-employed, the Revenue consider many factors which may include the following:

1. Does the business have your exclusive services?
2. Do you provide all or some of the tools or equipment required to do the work?
3. Are you free to decide the manner of working and time at which the work is done?
4. Are you taking a commercial risk and bearing expenses which could in some circumstances produce a loss?
5. Does any contract refer to you as self-employed or using a trading name?

# 9. Sole Trader

*What is a Sole Trader?*

A Sole Trader is a person who is in business on his own. The sole trader may have employees who are paid a salary, but unless those employees share in the profits *and* losses of the business, they cannot be regarded as partners in the business. The distinction between employees and partners is important for tax purposes. Great care must be taken to be sure that you know whether the people working with you are partners, employees or in some cases sub-contractors. This is particularly so because people use the word partner in everyday language to mean other things than a partner for tax purposes.

If you are the *only* person who:

(i) puts up the money for the business;
(ii) is entitled to the profits and losses of the business after deducting business expenses e.g. salaries and wages of employees other than yourself;
(iii) represents himself as owner of the business;

then you are definitely a sole trader, even if you employ your husband or wife in the business.


*How are the profits of a Sole Trader taxed?*

As described in Chapter 5, tax is charged under different Schedules and Cases which have their own tax rules. As a sole trader, the profits of the business are taxable under Schedule D Case I or Schedule D Case II. The distinction between Cases I and II is now fairly irrelevant as far as tax law is concerned. Case I relates to profits from trades and Case II relates to profits from a profession or vocation e.g. a lawyer or an accountant.

If you were an employee you would be taxable under Schedule E and the number of expenses which you could set against your earnings would be limited. To be able to deduct an expense under Schedule E you must prove that the expense is 'wholly, exclusively and necessarily' incurred for the purposes of your employment. Under Schedule D Case I and II the test is only 'wholly and exclusively' and the word necessarily does not apply.

A sub-contractor is not an employee, but another business, either sole trader, partnership or company and that other business does work for you. The sub-contractor invoices you for the work done and you pay that invoice. The expense being a business expense. If the sub-contractor and yourself are in the construction industry then a special tax deduction scheme applies. Then if the business supplying services to you does not have a sub-contractors tax certificate you may be liable to deduct tax at the basic rate from the payment to the sub-contractor. You would then have to pay the amount so deducted to the Inland Revenue. Full details about sub-contractors and sub-contractors certificates are given in Appendix VI.

The tax on the business profits of a sole trader is based on the annual accounts which are then adjusted to produce a taxable profit. Do not be confused between the accounting profit and the taxable profit. You may find that some bookkeepers or accountants will only prepare accounts for tax purposes. However, in order to judge how the business is doing from year to year you need accounts to be able to compare the profits and balance sheet prepared on a consistent basis.

From the business accounts you can prepare a tax computation which calculates how much of the business profits are taxable. A pro-forma computation is given in Appendix II at the back of the book. The actual amount of tax on the profit is calculated in your personal tax computation and will depend on your own personal situation. (That is, how much other income you have and how large your allowances such as personal allowances and mortgate interest relief are.) The rates of tax and allowances are published by the Revenue for each tax year. Ask for Revenue booklet IR21 and IR22 for the relevant tax year. A full list of free booklets is given in Appendix I.


## The Tax Computation

In arriving at an accounting profit you will have included all income of the business and deducted all expenses relating to the business. You will also have deducted such things as depreciation on fixed

43

assets (that is the cost, for one accounting period, of the use of the assets in the business). For tax purposes not all your expenditure is allowed as a deduction, and not all your income is necessarily taxable under Schedule D Cases I and II. In addition to this there may be certain tax allowances. It is to adjust for such items that the tax computation is prepared.

(a) The main types of expenditure which are not allowed as an expense and therefore must be 'added back' (that means the accounting profit must be increased by the amount of such expenses to calculate the taxable profit) are:

   (i) Entertaining (other than foreign customers).

   (ii) Legal fees relating to capital rather than trading matters such as fees relating to taking out a long lease on property, or for issuing new share capital.

   (iii) Expenditure which relates to your private rather than business affairs which may have been charged to the business account e.g. petrol, telephone, goods taken from a shop, your national insurance contributions.

   (iv) In preparing your accounts your salary or drawings from the business should not have been treated as an expense of the business, but if they have been then the salary is not allowed as a deduction.

     If the salary was allowed as a deduction, your income from the business would be split into two parts, (i) salary and (ii) profits. If you are a sole trader or partner there is no distinction between the two.

   (v) Losses on the sale of fixed assets which are dealt with in the Capital Allowance Computation.

   (vi) Depreciation.

(b) The main types of income which are not taxable with your trading profit and which must be deducted from your accounting profit in calculating your taxable income are:

   (i) Rental income from property which is taxable under Schedule A.

   (ii) Interest income which is taxable under Schedule D Case III.

   (iii) Profits on the sale of fixed assets. These are dealt with in the capital allowance computation and in certain circumstances may be subject to capital gains tax.

(c) The main types of tax allowances which reduce the accounting profit are:

(i)  Capital allowances. These are tax allowances which are a substitute for depreciation. The amounts and rates vary from time to time and may even vary in different parts of the country. For example, some special development areas will receive higher allowances than other areas. An outline of the structure of capital allowance relief is given below. To check the exact rates for a given year, please check in the Inland Revenue booklets in the CA series. The booklets are numbered CA1 to CA4 dependent on the allowance you are wanting to check.
CA1 Capital Allowances on machinery or plant.
CA2 Capital Allowances on industrial buildings.
CA3 Capital Allowances on agricultural or forestry buildings and works
CA4 Allowances for scientific research.
(ii)  Stock relief. This relief, which was originally introduced to take account of the inflationary cost of holding stocks, was withdrawn by the Finance Act 1984. It is no longer available for periods of account beginning after 12th March, 1984.

*Capital Allowances*

These tax allowances are given on certain capital expenditure instead of allowing depreciation.

Example:

| | |
|---|---:|
| Profit before Depreciation | £ 5,400 |
| Less: Depreciation | £( 400) |
| Accounting Profit | £ 5,000 |

| | |
|---|---:|
| In the tax computation: | |
| Accounting Profit | £ 5,000 |
| Add: Depreciation | £ 400 |
| | £ 5,400 |
| Less: Capital Allowances (say) | £( 540) |
| Taxable Profit | £ 4,860 |

Thus capital allowances are substituted for depreciation in calculating the taxable profit. The types of capital allowance available are:

Plant and Machinery allowances
Industrial Buildings allowances
Scientific Research allowances
Mines and Oil Wells allowances
Agricultural Buildings allowances

### (i) Plant and Machinery allowances

These are the allowances you would encounter most frequently, and for this reason people often refer to them as capital allowances. They are allowances for the cost of any asset or equipment *purchased* by you *for the purposes of your trade,* and which *belongs* to you at *sometime during the accounting period* in which the expenditure was incurred.

There are currently two types of allowance:

(i) A First Year allowance.
(ii) A Writing-down allowance.

The First Year Allowance is gradually being reduced to NIL with effect from 1st April, 1986 as described in Appendix III. The range of assets covered by the plant and machinery allowances is wide and will depend on the nature of the business you are carrying on. e.g. books are 'plant' for a lawyer or accountant. Office furniture and moveable partitioning is plant in an office environment. If you own or rent a shop the situation is not so clear cut. The shop front and lighting may not be regarded as plant while the counters and other fittings will be regarded as plant. Allowances are not available until the expenditure has been incurred and the interpretation of incurred sometimes gives difficulty. Assets bought on Hire Purchase are treated as belonging to you, and the expenditure is treated as being incurred, when the contract is signed.

When assets have been invoiced the expenditure is regarded as having been incurred on the invoice date, even though delivery may not have taken place.

The first year allowance, which is available in the year the expenditure is incurred, is not given if the asset is sold without being used or if the asset is purchased in the year in which the business ceases. The rate of allowance used to be 100%, but is being reduced gradually to NIL, which means that writing-down allowances start to become more significant.

The writing-down allowance is given on a reducing balance basis on the value of the 'pool of assets' at the end of the year. A basic

46

computation and detailed notes on capital allowances are given in Appendix III.

There are special rules for cars designed for conveying passengers, except where the trade is that of taxi-driver or car hire. Cars receive no first year allowance and a limited writing-down allowance. The writing-down allowance at present is the lower of 25% of the written-down cost or £2,000 – see Appendix III. Historically, the purchase of assets which attract first-year allowances has been used as a tax planning tool. Standard advice was to go and buy assets near your accounting year-end to reduce your taxable profit. That advice does not necessarily apply any more. It is imperative that you check the actual rates of allowances available and have a good estimate or your profit before considering the purchase of assets. If it takes 8 years to obtain tax relief on expenditure this makes the cost of acquiring the asset that much more expensive in cashflow terms than if relief is immediate. It may then make leasing preferable to buying the asset, although with lower capital allowances, the lease rates may be higher.

### (ii) Industrial Buildings allowances

Buildings which can be classified either as an industrial building or a hotel can receive allowances for their cost once in their lifetime. Thus, if the person who owned the building prior to you acquiring it has already been given a full complement of allowances on the building, none would be available to you. If the previous owner had received a part of the allowance then a proportion will be available to you. There are two allowances:

(i) An Initial allowance.

(ii) A Writing-down allowance

The initial allowance is given in the first year that the building is acquired and writing-down allowances are given in the first and subsequent years. The writing-down allowance is a fixed percentage of the original cost, or the residual value transferred to you when you buy the building; and thus you receive the same writing-down allowance each year until the whole cost of the building has been allowed. As with first year allowances initial allowance is gradually being phased out by 1st April, 1986. See pro-forma computation in Appendix IV. For example,

| Building Costs | £ 100,000 |
| Initial Allowance (say 50%) | ( 50,000) |
| Writing-Down allowance (say 4%) | ( 4,000) |
| Balance at end of year one | £ 46,000 |

All the allowances will have been given by the end of the thirteenth year. This method of giving allowances is unlike the reducing balance method used for plant and machinery allowances. In that instance the allowance reduces each year as the pool gets smaller.

The points to remember are that the rates of write-off are generally slow, and that unless you are the first owner of the building you may not receive any allowances at all. Shops, offices etc. receive no allowances. This makes office accommodation particularly expensive unless it is attached to an industrial site. Where offices form less than one tenth of the cost of the whole industrial building then allowances are available on the whole building costs including the office. There are special rules for small workshops. These are also being phased out. This is an example of a Government incentive being available for a limited period only.

### (iii) Scientific Research allowances

These allowances relate to all capital expenditure in connection with research projects. At present the allowance is 100% which means that all capital expenditure relating to scientific research may be deducted or 'written-off' in the year in which the money is spent.

### (iv) Mines and Oil Wells allowances

These allowances only relate to the coal mining industry and other extractive trades including the oil industry. It is not envisaged that anyone reading this book will wish to claim these allowances.

### (v) Agricultural Buildings allowances

These allowances are available to the owner of agricultural land who incurs capital expenditure on the construction of farm houses, farms buildings and works etc. There is an initial allowance and a writing-down allowance as described in the Revenue booklet CA3.

## When is the Tax Paid?

Working out when the tax on your accounting profits is actually due is one of the most confusing aspects of the tax system. It is worth a little effort in trying to understand the tax payment system so that you don't have the worry of when a brown envelope is going to drop through your letter box with an unexpected bill.

### (1) A Trade that has been going for some time

Tax is chargeable for tax years which run from 6th April in one year to 5th April in the next. e.g. 85/86 is the 6th April, 1985 to 5th April, 1986. If you have been trading for some time, the taxable profits for an accounting period which ends in one year are taxed in the next tax year. For example, Accounting period ended 30th June, 1985 ends in the tax year 85/86 and the profits for that period are taxed in the tax year 86/87. (This is known as the preceding year basis).

If you get confused by the dates it is best to draw a picture and put your dates on it, as shown below.

TAX
YEARS

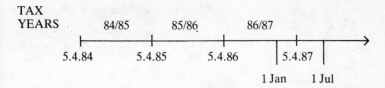

ACCOUNTING
PERIOD

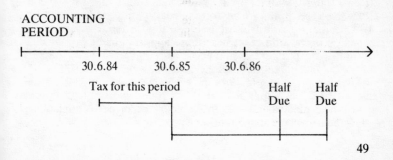

The actual rate of tax depends on other income and allowances for the 1986/87 tax year. The tax on the trading profit becomes payable, half on 1st January, 1987 and half on 1st July, 1987. These dates are known as the normal due dates. The tax may actually become due later if an assessment is under appeal as described in Chapter 4, but is never due before these dates.

You will be able to see that your accounting date can affect how long a gap there is between making the profit and paying the tax. If your year end was 31st March, the tax for the period 31st March, 1986 would be due on 1st January, 1987 and 1st July, 1987 a gap of 9 months to the first date. If the accounting date was 1 month later, 30th April, 1986 the due dates would be 1st January, 1988 and 1st July, 1988 giving a gap of 20 months.

## (2) Starting a Trade

When you start a trade, the Revenue don't want to wait until up to 20 months after the first accounting date to collect any tax and so they start collecting tax earlier. The year in which the trade starts is treated as the first tax year. e.g. start 1st January, 1985.

1st accounting date – 31st December, 1985

2nd accounting date – 31st December, 1986

3rd accounting date – 31st December, 1987

The first tax year is 1984/85 i.e the tax year into which 1st January, 1985 falls.

1984/85 – tax profits from start to 5.4.85

1985/86 – tax profits for 1st 12 months which is from the start to 31st December, 1985

1986/87 – year ended during the previous tax year or 1st 12 months again.

## General Commencement Rules

If you started business in 1985/86, then you would be taxed in 1985/86 on the profits arising from the date you started until 5-4-86. To calculate the profits attributable to this period, if accounts are prepared up to a different date, time apportionment is used. For example, start date 1st January 1986, first accounting date is 30-06-86. Taxable profits before capital allowances = £8,000.

The portion falling in 1985/86 is 3/6 x £8,000 = £4,000. In the case of first year allowances, these are deducted in the period in which the actual expenditure on the asset is incurred. Writing down allowances are time apportioned.

For the second year of assessment, 1986/87, the taxable profits are the adjusted profits for the first 12 months of trading (i.e. the profits from the date you started to 5-4-86 are effectively taxed for a second time).

The third year of assessment, 1987/88, would be based on the profits of the accounting period ending during 1986/87, unless those accounts are not for a full 12 months, in which case the first year of trading is assessed again. For example,

If you started business on 10th October 1985, and make up annual accounts to 30th June each year:

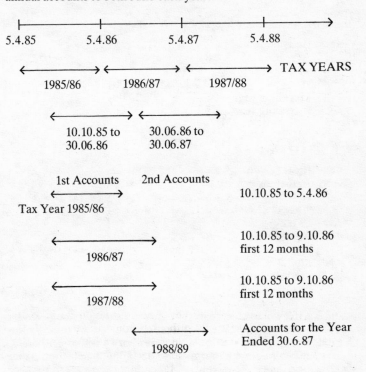

As the profits of the first year's trading may form the basis of assessment for the first three years, this may cause hardship where the profits are declining.

The taxpayer, therefore, has the option to elect under S.117 Income and Corporation Taxes Act 1970, that the taxable profits for the second and third tax years are on an actual basis. This has the effect of double taxing the profits in a later year. The claim must be made for both years, and must be made within seven years from the end of the second year of assessment of the business.

For example, ABC commenced business on 1st January 1985.

ABC earned an adjusted profit of:

£2,600 year to 31st December 1985
£2,000 year to 31st December 1986
£2,200 year to 31st December 1987

## Original Assessments

| Year | Basis Period | £ | £ |
|---|---|---|---|
| 1984/85 | Actual 1.1.85 - 5.4.85 | 650 | |
| | 3/12 x £2,600 | | |
| 1985/86 | 1st 12 months to 31.12.85 | 2,600⎫ | |
| 1986/87 | Preceding year to 31.12.85 | 2,600⎬ | 5,200 |
| 1987/88 | Preceding year to 31.12.86 | 2,000⎭ | |

## With a S. 117 Election

| Year | Basis Period | £ | £ |
|---|---|---|---|
| 1984/85 | Actual (as before) | 650 | |
| 1985/86 | Actual 6.4.85 - 5.4.86 | 2,450⎫ | |
| | 9/12 x £2,600 + 3/12 x £2,000 | | 4,500 |
| 1986/87 | Actual 6.4.86 - 5.4.87 | 2,050⎭ | |
| | 9/12 x £2,000 + 3/12 x £2,200 | | |
| 1987/88 | Preceding year (as before) | 2,000 | |

Thus, ABC would elect to pay on the reduced assessments under S.117, for 1985/86 and 1986/87, thereby, reducing the assessments by £700. Note that the election must cover both years or neither.

As a general rule, where profits are declining, an election under S.117 will be made. However, it is generally necessary to prepare both computations to see whether or not the election applies.

*Cessation*

On cessation, the year in which you cease trading is the last year of assessment for the business. Therefore, for example, if you ceased trading in 1987/88, the profits assessable in 1987/88 are the profits from 6th April 1987 until the date you ceased trading.

1987/88 – 6th April 1987 to date of cessation
1986/87 – Accounts for period ending in 1985/86
1985/86 – Accounts for period ending in 1984/85

However, the Revenue have the option to adjust to actual profits by time apportionment, if this would produce a higher assessable profit. For example,

A trader's adjusted profits are as follows:

| Years Ended 31st December | £ |
|---|---|
| 1983 | 4,000 |
| 1984 | 8,000 |
| 1985 | 6,000 |
| 1986 | 12,000 |
| 6 months to 30th June (when trading ceased) 1987 | 3,000 |

The original and final assessments for the last four years of trading would be as follows:

**Original Assessments**

| Year | Basis Period | £ | £ |
|---|---|---|---|
| 1987/88 | Actual 6.4.87 - 30.6.87 3/6 x £3,000 | 1,500 | |
| 1986/87 | PY - Y/e 31.12.85 | 6,000 | |
| 1985/86 | PY - Y/e 31.12.84 | 8,000 | 14,000 |
| 1984/85 | PY - Y/e 31.12.83 | 4,000 | |

**S.118 Revision**

| Year | Basis Period | £ | £ |
|---|---|---|---|
| 1987/88 | Actual as before | 1,500 | |
| 1986/87 | Actual 6.4.86 - 5.4.87 3/6 x £3,000 + 9/12 x £12,000 | 10,500 | |
| 1985/86 | Actual 6.4.85 - 5.4.86 3/12 x £12,000 + 9/12 x £6,000 | 7,500 | 18,000 |
| 1984/85 | PY - as before | 4,000 | |

As the revised aggregate assessments in this example result in larger taxable profits the Revenue would exercise its option to amend the assessments of 1985/86 and 1986/87 to an actual basis.

## *Trading Losses*

If your tax computation produces a tax loss then you may use this loss in a number of ways.
1. Claim the loss against total income in the year in which the loss is sustained or in the succeeding year.
2. Carry the loss forward against future profits of the same trade.
3. If the loss arises in the first 3 tax years of assessment of the trade, then the loss may be carried back against the individual's other income in the three years preceding the commencement starting with the remotest year first.

   For example: Trade commences 1 January 1985. Loss incurred in the period to 30th June 1985 = £10,000. 1985/86 assessment = NIL. The £10,000 may be carried back against total income arising in 82/83 then 83/84 then 84/85.

Care needs to be taken in making such a claim, because it could reduce the income in the earlier year to NIL, thus losing the benefit of personal allowances and mortgage interest relief.

## *Value Added Tax*

Value Added Tax (VAT) was introduced in 1973 to replace purchase tax. It is a tax administered by the Customs and Excise rather than the Inland Revenue. It is thus based on a seperate piece of legislation with different interpretation and administration from other taxes.

VAT is chargeable on all goods and services supplied by taxable persons. Taxable persons are individuals, partnerships, companies etc. who are or should be registered for VAT.

### Registration

When you start up in business or if you are already in business, and are not yet registered for VAT you need to decide whether registration is required now or in the future. If you are already registered for VAT, you need to be aware of de-registration requirements.

Anyone who is carrying on a business which has a taxable turnover above certain limits is a taxable person and must notify Customs and Excise. You cannot escape registration by splitting your business into several parts trading under different names. If the total turnover of the several businesses together exceed the limits then you are liable to register.

Taxable turnover means the total value of sales of goods or services made by you in your business, not just the profit you make. For example, if you are a retailer then your taxable supplies are the sum of all sales and the market value of any goods taken by you for your own use from the shop. If you are a plumber, your taxable supplies are the sum of all invoices for supplying plumbing and related services.

The registration limits change in the budget each year, and you therefore need to check with the VAT office what the limits are. Also the Treasury has power to increase these limits by Statutory Instrument, which means that an Act of Parliament is not required. The limits set by the Finance Act 1984 are given in Appendix VII.

If you are not required to register compulsorily, then you may like to consider whether voluntary registration would be beneficial. Voluntary registration is possible, but Customs and Excise are now more strict in the terms on which they allow voluntary registration.

The advantages of voluntary registration are:
1. If your business is small you may wish people to think your turnover is larger than it actually is. This is done by registering and charging VAT. Once registered, people will assume your turnover is greater than the registration limits.
2. You are able to reclaim VAT on taxable supplies made to the business, such as petrol, stationery, telephone etc.

The disadvantages of registration are:
1. If the supplies of services are to the general public in a price competitive field then having to charge VAT could make you less competitive.
2. Your books of account must be kept in adequate form for VAT purposes, and you will be subject to periodic visits from VAT Inspectors.

If you decide you need to register, ring your local VAT office which will be listed in the telephone directory under Customs and Excise and say you want to register. They should send you a form VAT1 to be completed.

It is important to send in the Form VAT1 promptly. Registration takes effect from the date on which you become liable to be registered, and from that date you are liable to pay VAT on any taxable supplies you make in the course of your business, whether or not you have passed the charge on to your customers and whether or not you have notified Customs and Excise. There are penalties for failing to notify, and the effect of delay in notification may be that you may pay VAT on all your supplies without being able to recover any VAT on any supplies made to the business.

## Rates of VAT

All the goods and services which may possibly be supplied by business entities are classified by the rate of VAT if any which applies to those goods and services.

Goods and services may either be:

Exempt

Zero-rated

Standard-rated

If all your supplies are exempt, then there is no liability to register and no VAT paid by the business may be recovered. If the goods you supply are zero-rated, then you are in a favourable position. The rate of VAT charged on your supplies is NIL, but at the same time you may fully recover VAT you pay on supplies made to you for the business.

If you have a mixture of types of supply including exempt items such as food, then you have a situation called 'partial exemption'. This means that the relief for the VAT on supplies made to you is restricted. There are several methods by which this restriction may be carried out, and will often be the subject of negotiation with Customs and Excise.

If you are a retailer where partial exemption applies then one of the retail schemes may suit your business. These are designed to ease the accounting burden in calculating VAT. Care must be taken that you choose the correct scheme or else you could find you are paying over far too much tax. The scheme should be kept under review if the mix of goods changes.

## Making Returns and Keeping Accounts

Once registered you are liable to make quarterly returns, and pay over any associated VAT. These returns show (i) total VAT charged on goods and services in the quarter; this is termed VAT on OUTPUTS, (ii) total VAT paid on supplies of goods and services bought by you in your business; this is termed VAT on INPUTS. The difference is paid over to the Customs and Excise. If the VAT on INPUTS exceeds the VAT on OUTPUTS then a repayment is made. These payments and repayments are made automatically, no assessment or payment request is made. If, when a VAT Inspector calls, errors are found, then adjustments are made at that stage. As described in Chapter 3 of this book severe penalties for late returns and late payment of VAT as well as understatements of liability are being introduced in the 1985 Finance Act.

Accounts need to be kept showing VAT charged on all invoices raised by you and VAT claimed on all inputs borne by the business. A VAT account must be kept. Unless you have a mixture of exempt and standard or zero-rated supplies, then accounting for VAT is straight forward as long as good books of account are kept.

The most noteable items of INPUT VAT which cannot be recovered are:

(a) VAT on U.K. entertaining.

(b) VAT on company cars.


## Calculation of VAT on Goods and Services

Normally the VAT on an invoice is shown separately. e.g.

| | |
|---|---:|
| Goods | £ 10.00 |
| VAT @ 15% | £ 1.50 |
| Total | £ 11.50 |

Where it is not shown separately, you may wish to calculate how much VAT is included in the total paid; this is carried out as follows:

| | |
|---|---:|
| Goods | 100 |
| VAT | 15 |
| Total | 115 |

$\therefore$ VAT = 15/115 x TOTAL

## National Insurance

As a self-employed individual you are liable to pay two types of National Insurance.

1.  Class 2 National Insurance.

    This is a flat rate sum which must be paid either weekly or monthly. You can either stamp a card or pay by direct debit from your bank account. The rate for 85/86 was £4.75 per week and is being reduced to £3.50 per week from 6th October, 1985. For future years you can check the rate with the local DHSS office.

2.  Class 4 National Insurance.

    This is an amount payable on your taxable profits which fall between a lower and upper limit. The payment is collected by the Inland Revenue along with your income tax due on your trading profits. It is thus payable on 1st January and 1st July.

If you incur a loss in your trade and set the losses against the other income, then these losses may still be used for the purpose of the Class 4 National Insurance profits. In these circumstances the normal taxable trading profits may be different from the Class 4 National Insurance profits. With effect from 1985/86 onwards 50% of the Class 4 National Insurance contribution will be deductible from the individual's total income. This is to bring the contributions in line with the company position where much higher payments are fully deductible for corporation tax.

Example,

1983/84 Loss £4,000 which was set against other income.

1984/85 Taxable Profit £10,000

The Class 4 Profit is £10,000 − £4,000 = £6,000 `

The lower earnings limit for 1984/85 is £3,950

The upper earnings limit for 1984/85 is £13,000

Class 4 National Insurance due is £6,000 − £3,950 x 6.3 = 129.15

If the profit in 1984/85 had been £20,000 then the calculation would be:

Profit for Class 4 is £20,000 − £4,000 = £16,000

This means the maximum Class 4 contribution for 1984/85 is £570.15.

This is payable half on 1st January, 1985 and half on 1st July, 1985.

Neither Class 2 nor Class 4 National Insurance contributions qualify you for sickness benefit, or unemployment benefit, but they do qualify you for a pension.

If you have any employees, then you have to pay employers

National Insurance contributions as well as deducted employees National Insurance contributions from their salary along with any tax due under the PAYE system. The rates vary from year to year. The employer rate is 10.45% from 1-10-84 between certain limits. The upper earnings limit being £13,000. From 6th October, 1985 a new graduated rate is being introduced for employers with no upper earnings limit, this will greatly increase the burden of employing individuals on salaries above the upper earnings limit. The graduated scale is as follows:

| Weekly Earnings | Employers Rate |
|---|---|
| Below £35.50 | NIL |
| £35.50 - 55 | 5% |
| £55 - 90 | 7% |
| £90 - 130 | 9% |
| £130 above | 10.45% |

# 10. Partnership

Trading as a partnership is very similar to trading as a sole trader except that there is more than one of you sharing in the profits and losses of the business. It is normal and advisable to have a partnership agreement which is an agreement between the partners covering, among other things, the capital each will put up and the way the profits are to be shared. However, it is perfectly possible to act as partners and be taxed as partners without any formal written agreement.

When partnership accounts are made up the various tax adjustments are made as if the accounts were for a sole trader (see Chapter 9), then the taxable profit or loss is apportioned between the partners in their agreed profit shares.

The main difference between a partnership and a sole trader is that every time a partner leaves the partnership or a new partner joins, the old partnership is deemed to cease and a new one starts, so that the opening and closing year rules as described for a sole trader apply. If all the partners in the old and new partnership elect for the opening and closing year rules not to apply then the partnership is taxed as a continuing business. This is known as a continuation election.

The advantage of this rule in the past has been that with careful tax planning on partnership changes a whole year's income is not taxed while some years will be taxed twice. If the year that is taxed twice is a year of low profits, and the year that escapes tax is a year of high profits then considerable tax savings can be made. To counteract this considerable loss of tax to the Inland Revenue new rules are to be introduced in the Finance Act 1985. Where there is a change of partners and no continuation election applies, then the first 4 years of assessment following a change will be taxed on an actual basis i.e. on the profits arising in those 4 years instead of the normal opening rules. This will have a disincentive effect on changing partners purely for tax planning purposes.

If you have been trading as a sole trader for some time you may then decide to take in a partner. The same rules apply as if there was a partnership in existence and the number of partners had changed. You could either have a deemed cessation of the trade and a new trade commence, or you could elect to be taxed on a continuing basis. If a continuation election is made, then the new partner will have to pay tax on some of the profits you earned before he joined the partnership.

A partnership must register for VAT in the same manner as a sole trader. The VAT liability is that of the partnership as a whole, and any VAT not recovered is a partnership expense deductible from the total partnership profit.

# 11. Company

Trading through a company is very different from trading as a sole trader or partnership.

A company is a separate legal entity from its members (shareholders). While you may own shares in the company, it has an identity in its own right and even as a director and shareholder you work for it as an employee. There are two tax liabilities to consider:

1. that of yourself as an employee taxable under Schedule E or as a shareholder taxable on dividends paid by the company; and
2. that of the company subject to corporation tax.

*Taxation of yourself as employee or shareholder of the company*

If you are running the business through a company, it is likely that you are a director of that company. Director's earnings are taxed slightly differently from normal salaried employees.

(i) Benefits-in-kind, that is things paid for by the company which benefit you as an individual, are fully taxable irrespective of your salary level. Examples are:
   (a) Use of company car.
   (b) Travelling and entertaining.
   (c) Expense allowances.
   (d) Credit card facilities.
   (e) Use of accommodation or assets owned by the company.
(ii) The basis of taxation of your salary as a director may either be,
   Accounts basis or
   Earnings basis.
   These different bases apply instead of the normal basis for other employees because directors often take a small salary monthly and then wait and see what the accounting profit

looks like before voting themselves additional salary or bonus at the year end. It is in order to decide which tax year the additional earnings fall into for tax purposes that these different bases have evolved.

Accounts Basis:

Earnings arising in an accounting period of the company are taxable in the tax year in which the accounting period ends. For example Accounting period end 30th September, 1986 salary per the accounts is taxable in the tax year 1986/87.

Earnings Basis:

Earnings are apportioned on a time basis to the appropriate tax year. For example, if the Accounting period ends on 30th September, the earnings for the tax year 1986/87 would be made up by taking half the earnings for the period ended 30.9.86 and half the earnings for the period ended 30.9.87.

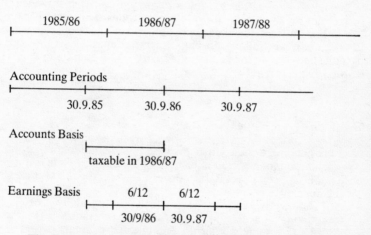

The Revenue prefer the accounts basis because it is easier to determine how much income is taxable. There is not a long time between the end of the tax year and the time when they will receive a set of accounts which will show them the taxable profit.

There are advantages of the accounts basis for the director because there is a deferral of the tax liability to some extent.

Strictly, the statutory earnings basis should apply to:

(a) the first year of assessment for which the emoluments are earned;

(b) the following year of assessment where the emoluments payable for the accounting period ending in the second year relate to a period of less than 12 months; and

(c) the year of cessation of the employment and the penultimate year.

Irrespective of the accounts or earnings basis, directors' earnings are subject to the PAYE regulations in terms of deduction of income tax and National Insurance at source.

Dividends received by you as a shareholder are part of your taxable income for the tax year in which the dividend is received from the company. Since the investment income surcharge has been abolished it would appear that there is little difference between salary and dividends received. However, the dividends are still investment rather than earned income and would not count as salary in calculating your entitlement to fund a pension. On the other hand, if your salary would be small in any case a dividend would not involve National Insurance liabilities. This point is particularly significant now the upper earnings limit has been removed from employers' National Insurance contributions. If the director is a married woman the receipt of a salary would qualify for wife's earned income relief whereas receipt by her of a dividend as a shareholder would just form part of her husband's taxable income.

## Taxation of the company

The tax liability of the company is based on the accounting profit for each accounting period adjusted in a similar way to that for a sole trader. Appendices I to III. Also see Revenue booklet CT1.

The main differences are:

(i) The opening and closing year rules do not apply. Corporation tax, payable on the profits of the accounting period, is due nine months after the end of the accounting period in question.

(ii) Your earnings from the company are fully deductible for corporation tax including any National Insurance that the company has to pay.

(iii) A company may set up a pension scheme for its directors and employees, and the contributions are fully deductible. A self-employed individual is only able to pay what are called 'Retirement Annuity Premiums'. These are a fixed percentage of the salary.

(iv) If you wish to take money out of the company other than as a salary, you may pay a dividend.

This dividend is being paid out of taxed income; that is income already taxed in the company. At the same time as paying the dividend the company must pay advance corporation tax. This advance corporation tax may be set against the corporation tax liability for the accounting period in which the dividend was paid. For the detailed rules relating to advance corporation tax see Appendix V. It may seem that it is better to pay dividends rather than salary because no National Insurance has to be paid but as outlined above the following matters must also be considered:

(a) Your state pension and unemployment benefit is based on your salary, if this is artificially low then those benefits will also be very low.

(b) The amount the company can contribute to a pension scheme is based on your salary. Your salary should not be so low as to make such contributions meaningless.

(c) Dividends are paid out of taxed income and are not a deduction from profits.

## The Rate of Corporation Tax

Corporation tax is fixed for tax years ended 31st March in arrears, although the rate has traditionally not changed a lot. There have been two rates dependent on the size of the profits. Unusually in the 1984 Budget the Chancellor of the Exchequer announced a reduction in the rate of corporation tax and fixed the rates for a number of years in advance. These rates are:

|  | Standard Rate | Small Companies | Marginal Rate |
|---|---|---|---|
| Year to 31st March, 1984 | 50% | 30% | 1/20 |
| Year to 31st March, 1985 | 45% | 30% | 3/80 |
| Year to 31st March, 1986 | 40% | 30% | 1/40 |
| Year to 31st March, 1987 | 35% | 30% | 1/80 |

The small companies rate applies to companies with profits up to £100,000 with marginal relief where profits are between £100,000 and £500,000.

Example of marginal relief.

| | |
|---|---:|
| Profits for year to 31st March, 1984 | £ 300,000 |
| | |
| CT @ 50% | £ 150,000 |
| Less Marginal Relief (500,000 - 300,000) 1/20 | ( 10,000) |
| | £ 140,000 |

Where the accounting period does not end on 31st March, then the taxable profits are time apportioned and the appropriate rates applied.

For example, year ended 31st December, 1986

| | |
|---|---:|
| Profits £ 800,000 | |
| 3 months to 31.3.86 £200,000 @ 40% | £ 80,000 |
| 9 months to 31.12.86 £600,000 @ 35% | 210,000 |
| Total | £ 290,000 |

## Value Added Tax

In a company, the VAT implications are the same as for a sole trader or partnership.

## National Insurance

In a company the National Insurance contributions are higher than for a sole trader, but they provide more benefits and the employer's contribution is deductible for corporation tax purposes.

Class 1 contributions are payable both by the employee and the employer. The employee's contribution is taken out of gross salary and both contributions are paid over to the Collector of Taxes under the P.A.Y.E. system.

For example, salary of £13,000

| | |
|---|---:|
| Employee's contribution | |
| £11,232 @ 9% | 1,010.88 |
| Employer's contribution | |
| £11,232 @ 10.45% | |
| = 1,173.74 after tax, say, | 821.62 |
| | £ 1,832.50 |

This is well over double the National Insurance due for a similar self-employed salary. From 6th October, 1985 this difference will become even larger. As outlined in Chapter 9 above the upper earnings limit for employers is to be removed, so that for employees earning over £13,000 the rate will be a fixed 10.45%, and in 85/86 the Class 4 contribution paid by a self-employed individual will be 50% tax deductible.

# 'Decision Making'

This third section of the book deals with a few of the major business decisions that you are likely to have to face. We have already stated that you should not allow tax implications to dictate your business decisions. However, you should always take the tax implications into account.

We hope this book will make you more aware of how taxation fits into the context of your business. Then when you are making decisions you will at least consider the likely tax effects.

In purely financial terms a choice between two courses of action should be judged on the respective results anticipated after rather than before tax.

# 12. Decision making and tax implications

We have now covered in some detail the Income Tax and Corporation Tax treatment of different businesses depending on the type of legal entity you have selected. You should have some idea of the application of such taxes to your business. You should also know what you have to do to comply with the administrative aspects of tax for your own business.

One of the most rewarding and refreshing times in the career of a tax specialist is when he first has to consider the tax system of a foreign country. You tend to assume that some basic structural aspects of our tax system cannot be changed. Then you find that in other countries those 'basic' points do not even exist. If you are left to explain our system to a foreign tax expert you start to focus on those aspects of a tax system that are common.

For example, in the UK we have Capital Transfer Tax which is a gifts tax or death duty. This tax is assessed on the person making the gift or in the case of property passing on death it is assessed on the estate of the deceased. In some other countries there is no such tax but instead there is an Inheritance Tax whereby an individual is taxed on the receipt of a gift and on the receipt of property passing to him on the death of another person.

The common link therefore, in this example, is not the type of tax but the transaction or event which triggers a tax liability. In both countries the relevant transaction is the making of a gift or the passing of property on death and the relevant event is the death.

Taxation usually occurs in relation to a transaction or an event. Sometimes the event relates to a value. For example, making a profit below a specified amount might make available a special allowance reducing the tax liability.

Where does this leave you and your business? Well, in running your business you are continually making decisions. These decisions are often about transactions or could result in events taking place most of which will have tax implications. You should be aware of the tax treatment of your regular business transactions and of the extent to which your trading profit or loss is likely to be reflected by the profit or loss for tax purposes.

You should therefore be alert when you are making any significant decisions outside your normal course of business. Examples of such decisions could relate to any of the following:

1. Capital expenditure.
2. Change of business premises.
3. Provision for Pensions.
4. Borrowing.
5. Investment of surplus funds.
6. Planning new products.
7. Diversification.
8. Foreign activities.

These are just a few examples of decisions relating to significant transactions or events which are bound to involve serious tax considerations. Focus on the decision you are trying to make or the transaction you may be entering into. Will it involve income or expenditure or both? Will it be in the nature of a trading transaction or more of a capital transaction? How are the Revenue likely to treat the income or expenditure? Could the same business objective be achieved by any other means?

You may well be unable to answer any of those sort of questions but do try. Then at least you can seek advice from a position of strength in that you will have focused on the actual nature of the transaction. All too often tax specialists jump to conclusions as to the nature of transactions or the character of certain items of income or expenditure. At least, before you seek advice, try to get the facts straight. That will avoid fees for unnecessary work by your advisors. If you are planning to acquire another business it could have a significant effect if it were a company rather than a business of a sole trader. If you are buying a company, is it the shares you are buying, or is it the trade, or is it just some of the assets? If you are 'buying' a property is it freehold or leasehold?

Sort out the facts that you think are significant and try to judge the tax impact. Then when you speak with your advisors you have a better chance of understanding their advice.

In the remaining Chapters of this book we look at some of the major business decisions. Without being too specific, (since this is not a textbook) we suggest how you should approach the tax aspects or implications of each decision.

There is one obvious way to alert yourself to a possible tax problem. Set out clearly your business plan and budget for each year. Try to include tax as an integral part of that budget. In order to do that you must therefore have considered the tax treatment of all the income, expenditure, borrowing and distribution aspects of your budget. Then, on an exception basis, if anything arises that is not included in your budget, or if the value of the items changes you should immediately consider whether those changes have any significant tax implications.

# 13. The financing or borrowing decision

The basic aim in borrowing for or financing a business is to obtain
the funds at the lowest possible cost. That cost may range from
legal costs, through loan interest costs to actually sacrificing a share
in the business. The decision usually involves a choice between
different interest rates. However the tax deduction or relief
available for such interest expense is crucial in deciding which
available source of finance is the cheapest in after tax terms. The
first occasion when this decision is usually faced is at the start-up of
the business.

## Set-up

The actual timing of the start of a business is often largely a matter
of chance. An event such as redundancy or a chance of a particular
business property coming on the market are often the sort of
unexpected event which triggers a business being set up. Suddenly
being offered one large contract or deal is another frequent yet
unpredictable cause.

In other cases where plans have been made and a date set to start
the business there is usually some reason why that date is delayed.
If the timing is a matter of chance so too will be your financial
position when it happens. You may have the capital available to
buy or to fund the business but should you put that money into the
business or should you borrow elsewhere.

At this initial stage of funding the business it is very important to
look at your overall personal financial position. What other forms
of borrowing do you have or do you need? Are you obtaining tax
relief for all your current borrowing? For example you may have a
mortgage, the capital value of which is above the £30,000 limit for
tax relief on interest to be available. At the same time you might
have some capital (such as redundancy money) which you plan to
put into the business. This provides two possibilities;

1. Borrow separately to fund the business. In most cases you should be able to obtain tax relief for such borrowing. That is true even if you are operating through a limited company. If you borrow yourself and lend the funds to the company then you should be able to obtain tax relief on the interest payments (depending on the size of your holding in the share capital of the company.) Then you can use the funds to repay that part of the mortgage that does not attract loan interest relief. If you are uncertain about the amount of funds required for the business you may decide to delay repayment of the mortgage for a few months.
2. Leave the mortgage as it is and lend the redundancy money to the business.

This second option is obviously less favourable as part of the interest expense is not relievable for tax purposes. Option 1 would normally be chosen.


*Running the business.*


The cost of finance is obviously a decision based on relative interest rates but you should always look at those interest rates on an after tax basis. Bad debts may be a problem in your business depending on the volume of customers and how well you know them. You may well try to improve your cash flow by giving discounts for prompt payment. If it is only a question of time before your customers pay, rather than a real bad debt risk then be careful to compare overdraft or loan interest rates after tax with what might be an expensive way of borrowing through giving over-generous discounts.

In any financing decision the objective must be to obtain tax relief as far as possible for the costs of obtaining the finance. Although that seems obvious the tax relief may not be of any great value if you have accumulated trading losses for tax purposes. In that situation perhaps you should be looking at increasing the equity of the company rather than borrowing more funds.


*Expansion of business*


The same basic tax points apply in funding the expansion of a business. Your options of available finance may well be restricted by the particular circumstances of your business at the time. Once again you should widen your choice by reviewing your personal financial position.

If your personal situation has changed consider whether the most cost effective method of borrowing is through your own resources or for the business to borrow directly from a bank or other source of finance.

You may have established a pension fund which could prove to be a worthwhile source of finance. Another method of obtaining finance might be to consider leasing rather than outright purchase of fixed assets. Factoring your business debts might also be considered. In all these cases however you must look at the effective after-tax cost of the finance in deciding which is the cheapest source of funds.

Tax should therefore be a basic part of the financial comparison of interest costs but, as ever, the financial aspects may not be dominant. Even if factoring your business debts appeared to be the cheapest source of finance after taking account of tax you may not wish to take that course for non-financial reasons. For example you might feel that it would be bad for the image of your business or that it might alienate some of your customers.

In some cases you might seek finance for expansion by taking on a partner or by selling shares in the business to another party. This may seem a cheap method of raising funds depending, of course, on the price paid by the new partner. You may still retain control of the business or company in terms of votes. However such a move might seriously impede your flexibility in terms of tax planning.

Whereas previously you might have reduced the tax liability of the business by voting yourself additional salary or pension contributions the existence of a new partner might restrict that flexibility. That is an important factor from the point of view of tax. It may be the flexibility you are sacrificing that enables you to make decisions which help to minimise your tax liabilities.

# 14. Capital expenditure decisions

Expenditure on fixed assets for a business is not usually a regular occurrence. It is also likely to involve significant amounts of money. One further aspect is that it often involves replacement of an existing fixed asset and therefore the acquisition may also be the occasion of a disposal of some other fixed asset.

Acquisitions and disposals of fixed assets are the type of transaction we have previously referred to in this section of the book. They may be exceptional items not necessarily included within your budget for the period.

You should consider the following tax points when deciding between different assets and how to pay for them.

1. Is the particular asset of a type such that the expenditure on its acquisition will qualify for capital allowances? The detailed rules about capital allowances have been referred to in the second section of this book.

2. If capital allowances are available will this affect the cost of the asset? If you have accumulated trading losses for tax purposes it may be that the capital allowance deduction just adds to that loss. In such a case you would be fooling yourself if you assumed that the capital allowances effectively reduced the cost of the asset. The present value of the capital allowance deduction may not therefore be very significant.

3. If you cannot use the capital allowances at present would it be more effective to lease the asset rather than to purchase it directly? The system of leasing leaves the ownership of the asset with the leasing company during the period of the lease. The leasing company therefore has the benefit of the capital allowance deduction and that is reflected in the cost of leasing making it usually more attractive than other forms of borrowing. The gradual reduction in the rates of capital allowances introduced by the 1984 Finance Act will increase the relative cost of leasing when compared to other forms of borrowing. That is because the tax deduction available to the leasing companies is being reduced or at least delayed.

77

4. If you are trading through a limited company or partnership would it be beneficial to acquire the asset personally and then charge the business for the use of the asset? One example might be the acquisition of business premises. That may be a long term investment. It is likely to be an asset that will increase rather than diminish in value. There are unlikely to be any capital allowances available for such expenditure.

Business premises provide good security for a loan and therefore, depending on your own financial position you may be able to borrow a significant proportion of the cost. The loan interest could be deducted from the rental income in your personal tax computation and that may mean there is no increase in your personal taxable income in the early years of the loan.

5. Could your pension fund acquire or finance the acquisition of the asset? Again, as in 4. above this may be of greatest relevance in the case of business premises. Some pension funds could be used as sources of loan-back to the individual to assist in the purchase under 4. above. If you have a self-administered pension fund the fund itself could acquire the premises and rent them to the company. Obviously the trustees must compare this investment with the likely return from other forms of investment for the pension fund. They could not allow one asset to represent too large a proportion of the total investments of the fund. However, if it was an acceptable form of investment it would certainly be efficient from a tax point of view. The rental payments would be a deductible expense in the Corporation Tax computation of the company. The pension fund would receive the rental income and any capital growth in the value of the asset free of tax.

We have covered certain tax aspects of the decisions for the acquisition and financing of fixed assets. The other important point to consider is the timing. As we mentioned earlier, when you acquire an asset it often replaces an older asset which is then disposed of by the business. You may look at trading the old asset in for the new one though you may feel you could obtain a discount on the new asset and do better to sell the old asset separately. If you are trading the old asset in then you do not have much choice of timing since the sale and purchase would be concurrent.

If you do have a choice in timing and it is near your accounting date you may wish to delay disposing of the old asset until after the accounting date. It is likely to be beneficial to acquire the new asset before the accounting date. It is difficult to generalise. The basic point is that you should have an estimated tax computation available to see the capital allowance and possible capital gains implications of these transactions. You can then judge the preferable timing if you have a choice. Although the immediate value of capital allowances is being reduced you should still try to evaluate fixed asset acquisitions and disposals in after-tax terms.

# 15. Pension provision

Many businessmen never want to give up the reins and leave the business they have created. The image is usually given that they could not bear to retire because they enjoy their work so much. Doubtless that is true in many cases but for many others they cannot afford to stop working.

Assume you will wish to retire at a given age (say 60) then review each year how you are going to live and what financial provision you have made to ensure you will have a sufficient income at that time. It must depend, of course, on the type of business you are in, and whether your children are likely to succeed to the business.

If, like a consultant, the business goodwill entirely relates to yourself then you are unlikely to be able to sell the business and when you stop working the business will most likely come to an end. If, like a farmer, you are in a capital intensive business then, if your children do not wish to farm you may be able to plan to sell the farm land and buildings when you want to retire.

If your situation is like that of the consultant above you need to make some financial provision for your old age. If you are in a business like that of the farmer above you may feel that the assets or goodwill of the business will be able to yield sufficient funds to keep you when you retire.

Your business could fall anywhere in a range between the two extremes given. You should assess your own likely position and then decide what to do. Starting a pension fund is not necessarily the only answer. As mentioned in the previous chapter you might consider investing personally in business premises and renting them to your business. That would give you a (hopefully) appreciating and income producing asset and might put you closer on the scale towards the farmer rather than the consultant.

However, when you take account of the tax treatment of pension provision direct personal investment producing taxable income may not appear very efficient. Pensions are one example of the Government using the tax system to provide an incentive to further its social and economic policies. The Government does not want to have to shoulder the entire financial burden of providing for people in their old age. In its policies it therefore encourages individuals to make their own provisions. Of course you could just save a part of your income ready for your retirement but, if you do, the income generated by those savings will be taxed in the intervening years. The accumulated savings are therefore likely to be lower than if they could have been accumulated free of tax.

The basic principles governing the tax treatment of pension policies or pension funds are therefore as follows:

1. Within certain generous limits money committed to approved pension schemes is allowed as a deductible expense for tax purposes either for the individual's income tax or, in the case of company contributions for Corporation Tax.

2. Money, once paid to such a pension fund cannot be repaid until normal retirement age except in unusual circumstances of early retirement for health reasons.

3. The pension funds can accumulate free of any income tax or capital gains tax. The only exception would be if the activities of the fund were such as to constitute a form of trading for income tax purposes.

4. The pension when received is based on a purchased annuity. Part of the pension will represent capital repayment and will be tax free. The income part of the pension will be taxable as earned income.

An individual who saved during his working life could also purchase an annuity with his savings when he reaches retirement age. However none of the taxable part of the annuity income could be treated as earned income. That may be less important now that the income tax rates are the same for both earned and unearned income. It could however be significant for a married woman for whom wife's earned income relief would be available against a pension which she has provided for during her own working life.

If you are a sole trader or a partner in a partnership you have a choice of many different insurance companies' pension policies. This is not the place for a discussion of which one you should select. The tax treatment is not one of the distinguishing features between the different policies. The only tax point is not which one to select but how much to put into the pension. There are limits based on your taxable income. However the limits are generous and if you are just starting to provide for a pension you may be able to pay some premiums relating to your income in earlier years.

If you are a company director running your own business you

have more choice as to the type of pension scheme available. You also have a choice whether it should be funded by payment from yourself of from the company or from both. If the amounts the company can afford to pay as pension contributions are substantial it may be worthwhile for the company to establish a truly self-administered pension fund. It requires an independent trustee and actuarial advice. One of the main advantages is that the pension fund can lend funds back to the company more easily than from an insured fund where there are often substantial costs involved. Also, if you later want to start another business the pension fund could invest in it or lend funds to the new business.

# 16. Change of Trading Entity or Closing Down the Business

In the second section of this book we have already dealt with the different types of business entity. We have also explained the implications of changing from being a sole trader to taking on a partner. In this section of the book we are dealing with tax aspects of making business decisions. In most cases you have freedom to decide the timing of a change of business entity or the timing of closing down a business.

It is this decision on timing that is the significant decision for tax purposes. If you go bankrupt or your company is put into receivership or liquidation then you may have little choice. If you are selling the business or the business assets again a third party is involved. That may reduce your flexibility in relation to timing.

The more likely case is that you are running down the business either because you wish to retire or because you want to devote your efforts to another business or occupation.

Along with the many other factors involved in such a decision you should consider the following tax implications.

1.  Under the rules of Schedule D Cases I and II for sole traders and partnerships special rules apply for the closing years of a business. The profits will normally have been taxed on a preceding year basis, as described in Chapter 9.
    Whereas under opening year rules the tax payer can elect to be taxed on the actual profits if that is beneficial, under the closing year rules the Revenue have the right to change the basis of assessment to tax the actual profits in the final years if that increases the tax liability. If the profits are rising in the final years the Revenue will usually alter the basis of assessment to actual. Clearly, if you have time to plan for the closing down of your business you could gradually reduce the level of trading if that has the effect of reducing your taxable profits over the final three years.

2. A general point you should consider is whether you have accumulated tax losses which will not be used on closure of the business. This can apply for any type of trading entity. Can you therefore time the closure of the business to coincide with using up these tax losses?

   Equally, if you have paid tax on profits of the business in recent years you should consider whether there is any way of obtaining a repayment of some of that tax. Once again the timing of closure of the business and controlling the level of trading in the final years may provide losses which could be carried back to obtain such a repayment.

3. If you are able to time the closure of the business you should also consider the timing of disposal of individual business assets. You should estimate the likely disposal proceeds and the related effect on capital allowances and the likelihood of chargeable capital gains occurring. Once again, the timing of such asset disposals may have a significant effect depending on; in which accounting period or in which tax year disposal takes place.

4. If you intend to start or continue another business after the closure of this particular business you should look closely at the likely capital gains, if any. Depending on the nature of the assets disposed of and the types of new assets required for the other business you may be able to avoid an actual capital gains tax liability. Roll-over relief is available in some circumstances so that the new assets can be treated as having been acquired at the original cost of the old business asset. The capital gain on the old asset is then effectively deferred by being rolled-over with the eventual gain on the disposal of the new asset. No capital gains tax would then be payable until the disposal of the new asset.

5. One further capital gains point to consider is Retirement Relief. In the 1985 Budget the Chancellor of the Exchequer extended the scope of this relief. It effectively exempts from the charge to capital gains tax the first £100,000 of gains accruing on the disposal of chargeble business assets. Clearly, on retirement, no roll-over relief (as described in 4 above) would be available. Retirement relief previously applied where the gains accrued to a person retiring at the age of 65 or over, with some reduced relief between the ages of 60 and 65. The Chancellor has proposed that the full relief should now be available from the age of 60 and that it also should be available to individuals before that age if they are forced to retire on medical grounds.

The disposal or closure of your business may come about on the occasion of your death. In such a case you will hopefully have anticipated the situation in terms of preparing a will and planning to some extent for the possible Capital Transfer Tax liabilities that might ensue. One of the benefits of a disposal on the occasion of death is that it does not constitute a disposal of assets for the purposes of Capital Gains Tax.

In relation to Capital Transfer Tax there is also some provision for relief from the tax in relation to business assets. This business property relief is given in the form of a reduction in the value of the relevant business property transferred. If the particular property qualifies under the provisions of section 105 of the Capital Transfer Tax Act 1984 relief will be available as a reduction of 50% or 30% in the value transferred. The rate varies depending on the type of business asset. The asset cannot be a qualifying business asset for this purpose unless you have owned it for the two years preceeding its transfer.

# 17. Decisions on the use of Surplus funds

These decisions present problems for any business but they are more obvious in the case of a limited company. In a company the Board of Directors have to make positive decisions if they intend to distribute or reinvest surplus funds. Just to keep the funds in the company may not be the most efficient course of action although it may give a feeling of comfort if it reduces the need for the company to borrow. Possible uses of surplus funds include the following;

1. Investment in the expansion of the existing business.
2. Diversification into other types of business.
3. Passive investment of the funds.
4. Distribution of the funds to shareholders.
5. Increased pension provision.

In deciding which of these or other routes to adopt you should consider the tax implications. If the surplus is only a short-term situation then options 1 and 3 above may be the only prudent choices. We are really talking here about a situation where the medium term projections for the business show that it will generate cash surplus to its requirements. Assuming that these funds are really surplus in that sense we shall consider their application under each of the options above.

1. If there is still scope to expand the existing business you should consider the most tax effective way of doing this. The lowering of the rates of capital allowances has reduced the incentive to invest in capital equipment which provided 100% deductions in many cases. The scope to avoid or defer tax on such further investment will depend on the nature of the business and the timing of the investment.

2. Diversification can prove a commercial disaster if it diverts management time into unfamiliar activities. However, there may be more scope to improve your tax position by diversification than by expansion. If you have a seasonal trade you could diversify into a trade with a different seasonal peak. In the case of a sole trader the choice of accounting

dates for the two separate trades could have a significant tax effect. If your existing trade is producing surplus cash it is likely to be profitable for tax purposes. Starting a different business which might incur tax losses in its early years could therefore be a worthwhile move. If your business is paying tax then you can get immediate tax relief for any losses made in the new business. You therefore reduce your risk since the government is sharing the risk with you. If you are acquiring another business it may be therefore that your profitable position makes the new business effectively cheaper to you than to another purchaser who is not paying tax or who does not have an existing business. Alternatively that might be expressed in terms that you can afford to pay a higher price for that new business.

3. If you are considering the passive investment of surplus company funds in preference to its investment in trading activities you must consider whether that is the most efficient way to invest. It may be preferable to distribute the funds by way of increased salary or payment of a dividend to enable you as a director or shareholder to invest the funds personally. Alternatively the most tax efficient approach may be to put the funds into a pension scheme as described in Chapter 15. That will give a tax deduction in your presumably profitable company and will allow the income and capital gains on the investments to accrue free of tax in the pension fund.

You may not wish to go the pension route but prefer to have the funds more freely available. Then the choice is between investment by the company or by yourself. If gains on the investment accrue to the company you may find yourself effectively charged twice to capital gains tax. Your company will pay it once and then the gain will be reflected in the value of your shares in that company.

If you choose to distribute the funds and invest them personally there may be a tax cost in taking the funds out of the company. Clearly the decision must depend on the detailed tax position of both your company and yourself. The point we wish to make here is don't just leave the funds in the company for lack of a better idea. Always remember that you should review your personal tax position and that of the business at least annually and that review should include consideration of whether surplus funds are better invested by you personally or by your company.

4. Distribution of funds to shareholders has been covered in 3

above in relation to the investment of surplus funds other than in the business. You must compare the relative application of the funds inside or outside the company. Then you should evaluate the tax cost of making the distribution. You can then decide whether distribution of the funds is worthwhile.

5. Increased pension provision has also been dealt with in 3 above in relation to different choices for the investment of funds outside the business. The tax treatment of pension provisions and pension funds make this a course of action worthy of consideration even in the early years of a business.

# 18. Foreign Activities

So far in this book we have assumed that your business is conducted in the United Kingdom. However, in any tax planning you must consider whether the business or your own status introduce a foreign element to the tax situation.

The first point is your own tax status. If you are not Resident or not Domiciled (see Chapter 5) in the U.K. for tax purposes that could have a significant effect on your U.K. tax position. That ought to be taken into account when you first establish the business. If you are either non-Resident or non-Domiciled you should seek some advice in order to optimise the tax benefits that such status can provide.

The other important question is whether regardless of your own tax status, a lot of your business is conducted outside the U.K. or if your business is largely concerned with foreign customers or foreign suppliers.

Even if you feel confident in understanding your U.K. tax position do not assume that you can apply the same tax principles in another jurisdiction. The choice of business entity that you have made in the U.K. may be totally unsuitable for doing business in another country. Take advice or enquire as to the tax laws which will affect you in the other country. Plan ahead and predict the likely foreign tax liabilities which you may incur.

You may find it advantageous to trade in the foreign country using a different type of legal entity. For example, a sole trader might find it worthwhile to form a company abroad through which to conduct his overseas purchasing or selling. That new entity might be established in a third country other than the U.K. or the country in which you are doing business.

It would be unfair if you had to pay tax on the same income in two different countries. The U.K. therefore allows tax relief for foreign tax paid in most circumstances. This is usually governed by the terms of Double Tax Treaties made between the U.K. and individual countries. These Treaties can vary in scope and it is best to consult the Treaty for the particular country in which you plan to do business. The terms of the treaty can affect the way you do business in that country as well as the choice of legal entity to use for such business.

If there is no Treaty, relief may still be available for foreign tax paid when computing your U.K. tax liability. Unless double tax relief was available there would be a significant disincentive to foreign trade.

# Tax and Financial Planning Ltd.

This company was founded in 1979 by the authors of this book, Anne Lavies and Gordon McClure. The main objective in founding the company was to develop computer software for tax applications.

The company was initially funded by the provision of tax consultancy services, which continue to expand as a major part of the company's activities. However, significant development work has been undertaken to produce a comprehensive Income Tax system running on personal micro computers.

Tax software development work continues and the company is now marketing tax software packages to accountants, banks and other tax advisers. In the last year the company has been expanding its Personal Tax consultancy services using its own computer systems. This makes personal tax work cost effective and profitable while enabling the company to provide fixed quotes for Tax Return work and at the same time a better quality of service.

The company is based in Woking at:

Barratt House,
7 Chertsey Road,
Woking,
Surrey,
GU21 5AB.
Telephone (04862) 5781

# Appendix I

*List of Revenue Booklets which are useful Guides to U.K. Income Tax and Capital Gains Tax*

It is important that you also obtain the latest supplement or update, as many of the tax rates and allowances will be out of date in these booklets, although the explanation of the principles will be correct.

| NUMBER | DATE | TITLE |
|---|---|---|
| **IR Series** | | |
| IR(Insert) | (1983) | Income Tax and Capital Gains Tax rates and allowances, 1983/84 |
| (BP | (1983) | Budget Proposals 1983) |
| IR1 | (1980) | Extra-statutory concessions |
| IR1(Supp) | (1981) | Extra-statutory concessions |
| IR1(Supp) | (1982) | Extra-statutory concessions |
| IR1(Supp) | (1983) | Extra-statutory concessions |
| IR4 | (1984) | Income Tax and pensioners |
| IR4A | (1983) | Age Allowance |
| IR6 | (1978) | Double Taxation Relief |
| IR9 | (1979) | Notes on treatment of livestock kept by farmers and other traders |
| IR11 | (1974) | Tax treatment of interest paid |
| IR11(Supp) | (1977) | Tax treatment of interest paid |
| IR12 | | (1979)Occupational pension schemes |
| IR13 | (1984) | Wife's Earnings Election |
| IR14/15 | (1983) | Construction Industry Tax deduction scheme |
| IR16 | (1974) | Share acquisitions by Directors and employees |
| IR16(Supp) | (1977) | Finance Act 1976 Supplement |
| IR18 | (1979) | Corporation tax |

| NUMBER | DATE | TITLE |
|---|---|---|
| IR47 | (1982) | Income Tax: Deed of Covenant by parent to adult student |
| IR51 | (1983) | The Business Expansion Scheme |
| IR52 | (1984) | Your Tax Office: Why it is where it is. |
| IR53 | (1984) | PAYE for employers: Thinking of taking someone on? |

## CA Series

| CA1 | (1973) | Capital Allowances on machinery or plant |
|---|---|---|
| CA1(Supp) | (1977) | Finance Act 1976 supplement |
| CA2 | (1972) | Capital Allowances on industrial buildings |
| CA2(Supp) | (1979) | Finance Act 1978 supplement |
| CA3 | (1980) | Capital Allowances on agricultural or forestry buildings and works |
| CA4 | (1973) | Allowances for scientific research |

## CGT Series

| CGT1 | (1971) | Capital Gains Tax: how to calculate your gains |
|---|---|---|
| CGT2 | (1980) | Capital Gains Tax: quoted shares and securities |
| CGT4 | (1983) | Capital Gains Tax: owner-occupied houses |
| CGT5A | (1972) | Capital Gains Tax: unit and investment trusts |
| CGT6 | (1979) | Capital Gains Tax: retirement: disposal of a business |
| CGT7A | (1971) | Capital Gains Tax: individuals: treatment of assets on death |
| CGT8 | (1980) | Capital Gains Tax |
| CGT8(Supp) | (1981) | Finance Act 1980 supplement |
| CGT8(Supp) | (1982) | Finance Act 1981 supplement |
| CGT10 | (1975) | Capital Gains Tax: development gains from land and first letting charge |
| CGT11 | (1983) | Capital Gains Tax and the small businessman |

| NUMBER | DATE | TITLE |
|---|---|---|
| CGT12 | (1983) | Capital gains tax. Indexation: Finance Act 1982 |

**CTT Series**

| | | |
|---|---|---|
| CTT1 | (1983) | Capital transfer tax |

**DLT Series**

| | | |
|---|---|---|
| DLT2 | (1982) | Development land tax |
| DLT30 | (1982) | Development land tax: notices of disposals |

**P Series**

| | | |
|---|---|---|
| P5 | (1983) | Farmer's guide to PAYE |
| P5(Supp) | (1984) | Farmer's Guide to PAYE |
| P5(Supp 2) | (1984) | Farmer's Guide to PAYE |
| P7 | (1983) | Employer's guide to PAYE |
| P7(Supp) | (1984) | Employer's Guide to PAYE |
| P7(Supp 2) | (1984) | Employer's Guide to PAYE |
| P7 | (Master) | Master's Guide to the marine tax deduction (1977) scheme |
| P(Seaman) | Seaman's Guide to the marine tax deduction (1973) scheme | |

**Other Pamphlets**

| | | |
|---|---|---|
| 46Q | (1983) | Returning payments in the entertainments industry |
| 480 | (1984) | Notes on expenses payments and benefits for directors and certain employees |
| Miras 6 | (1982) | Mortgage interest and your tax relief |
| Miras 7 | (1983) | Loan interest and tax relief |

# Appendix II

*Pro-forma tax computation for schedule D case I and II*

**NOTES**

| | | | |
|---|---|---|---|
| Profits as shown in your profit and loss or trading account | | | P |
| | ADD: (certain items if included in the figure P) | | |
| | Depreciation on Fixed Assets | £ x | |
| 1 | Losses on the disposal of Fixed Assets | x | |
| 2 | Entertaining (except foreign customers) | x | |
| 3 | Disallowed subscriptions/donations | x | |
| 4 | Disallowed Legal and Profes-sional fees | x | |
| 5 | Other disallowable expenditure | x | |
| 6 | Disallowance for Proprietor's use of assets and stock | x | |
| 7 | Bad Debt Provision (General Reserve) | x | |
| | | | D |
| | LESS: | | |
| 8 | Income chargeable separately, e.g. interest income, rental income | x | |
| 9 | Gains on the sale of Fixed Assets | x | |
| 7 | Reduction in Bad Debt Provision (General Reserve) | x | |
| | | | (–)L |
| | Taxable Schedule D Case I or II income | | X |
| 9 | Stock Relief | | (-)SR |
| 10 | Capital Allowances | | (-)CA |
| | Taxable Income | | £ X |

# General Notes on the Adjustment of Profits for Tax Purposes

The pro-forma computation is given here by way of an example only, and is not intended to be exhaustive in its coverage.

The starting point for the computation is the profit (P) from the detailed trading, or profit and loss account. Items of expense included in the profit and loss account, which are not allowed as expenses for tax purposes, are 'added back' to the accounting profit (D). Income items which are not taxable under Schedule D Case I and II are deducted from the accounting profit (L).

The disallowed items fall into two main categories:

(a) expenditure which is of a capital nature;
(b) expenditure which is not incurred *wholly* and *exclusively* for trading purposes, e.g. private expenses.

In addition, there are certain expenses which are specifically disallowed, such as entertaining.

The term 'added back' is often used by accountants, and means that an item which has already been included as a deduction in arriving at a trading profit is added to that profit to calculate the taxable profit.

## Notes to Pro Forma Computation

1. The gains or losses on disposal of fixed assets are book gains and losses arising from selling an asset at a value, other than net book value.

   Example,

   | Cost of Asset | Accumulated Depreciation | Net Book Value | Sales Proceeds | Gain/ (Loss) |
   |---|---|---|---|---|
   | 100 | 75 | 25 | 30 | 5 |
   | 150 | 50 | 100 | 70 | (30) |

   The actual sales proceeds are used in the Capital Allowances computation. (See Note 10.)

2. Entertaining is specifically disallowed by the tax legislation, except in the case of entertaining an overseas-resident customer who does not trade in the U.K.
3. Subscriptions must be incurred wholly and exclusively for trading purposes, while gifts are specifically disallowed. A donation made to a charity after 1st April, 1980 is allowed as a trading expense

4. Legal and Professional Fees

These are normally allowed if they relate to the trade and do not relate to capital matters. Examples of capital items which would not be allowed are; alteration of the company's capital structure, advice on a new lease (rather than renewal of a lease), or advice on the acquisition of fixed assets.

5. Other Disallowable Expenditure

Examples of such items would be:

(a) personal expenses which are unrelated to the trade, but which you have not included in 6. below.

(b) Any general provisions made in the accounts.

6. Proprietor's Use of Assets and Expenses

In the case of unincorporated businesses there is a disallowance of the personal benefit the trader obtains from the use of premises, light, fuel, insurance etc., as well as a disallowance of any amounts that may have been taken from stock (at their *full retail value*).

7. General Reserves for Bad Debts

General Reserves for *any* expenses are not deductible for tax purposes, and must be added back in the computation. If a Reserve which has been made is subsequently written back in the accounts, the write back is not chargeable to tax. Bad Debt Reserves are the most common provisions for which adjustments have to be made for tax purposes. If you can satisfy the Inspector that the provision is against specific debts, rather than general, then it would be allowable as a deduction.

8. Income Chargeable Separately

Since income is taxed under separate Schedules, certain types of income should not be included with your Schedule D Case I or II income, but taxed separately. In particular, rents are taxed under Schedule A and interest income is taxed under Schedule D Case III. These items must be excluded from your Schedule D Case I or II assessable profit.

Schedule A income and Schedule D Case III income is included on your Tax Return separately.

9. Stock Relief

Stock relief was abolished by the Finance Act 1984 and is not available for periods of account which begin after 12th March, 1984. Any accounting period which straddles that date is treated as having come to an end on that date.

A pro-forma calculation of stock relief is as follows:

| Opening stock and work in progress | £ | B |
| LESS: de minimis deduction | | −2,000 |
| Amount to which percentage applied | £ | A |
| Apply percentage movement in stock relief index to A = Stock Relief | | x |

e.g. opening stock £10,000
Accounting Date 30-6-82
Percentage increase in all stocks index from 30-6-81 = 6.84
Stock Relief $(£10,000 − £2,000) \dfrac{6.84}{100} = £547$

## All Stocks Index

Recent values of the All Stocks Index, together with the percentage increase on the previous year are given below. The increases are to two places of decimals (the basis on which the stock relief scheme is administered).

| | 1982 | % inc. | 1983 | % inc. | 1984 | % inc. |
|---|---|---|---|---|---|---|
| Jan | 217.0 | 9.27 | 229.1 | 5.58 | 242.6 | 5.90 |
| Feb | 218.6 | 9.41 | 230.5 | 5.45 | 244.0 | 5.89 |
| March | 218.9 | 8.53 | 231.4 | 5.72 | 246.1 | 6.36 |
| April | 219.7 | 7.70 | 233.4 | 6.24 | N/A | |
| May | 220.6 | 7.35 | 234.4 | 6.26 | N/A | |
| June | 220.5 | 6.84 | 235.2 | 6.67 | N/A | |
| July | 221.1 | 7.08 | 235.5 | 6.52 | N/A | |
| Aug | 221.7 | 6.28 | 237.3 | 7.04 | N/A | |
| Sept | 223.0 | 6.25 | 238.7 | 7.05 | N/A | |
| Oct | 224.5 | 5.91 | 238.9 | 6.51 | N/A | |
| Nov | 225.3 | 5.73 | 239.1 | 6.13 | N/A | |
| Dec | 227.1 | 5.88 | 240.3 | 5.82 | N/A | |

# Appendix III

*Capital Allowances*

## 10. Plant and Machinery Including Motor Cars

### Pro-forma Computation

| Notes | Pool | Separate Pool | Expensive Cars | Capital Allowances |
|---|---|---|---|---|
| 1. Tax written down value b/fwd at beginning of accounting period | £ x | £ x | £ x | £ x |
| 2. Add: Transfer from connected persons | x | | | |
| 3. Motor Cars additions | | x | x | |
| | x | x | x | |
| 4. Less: Disposal Proceeds | x | x | x | |
| | x | x | x | |
| 5. Balancing allowance charge | x | x | x | x |
| | x | x | x | x |
| Less: Writing down allowance 25% | x | x | | x |
| 6. Writing down allowance expensive cars | | | x | x |
| | x | x | x | x |
| 7. Additions eligible for First Year Allowance (FYA) Plant and Machinery | x | | | |
| Commercial Vehicles | x | | | |

| Notes | Pool | Separate Pool | Expensive Cars | Capital Allowances |
|---|---|---|---|---|
| | x | | | |
| 8. Less: FYA claimed | x | | | x |
| | —— | —— | —— | |
| Written down value at end of accounting period | £ x | £ x | £ x | £x |
| | == | == | == | —— |
| Total Allowances | | | | £ x |
| | | | | == |
| Balancing charge | | | | £ x |
| | | | | == |

**Notes**

1. The tax written-down value brought forward at the beginning of the accounting period is obtained from the previous period's tax computation.

   **The Pool** includes all assets other than motor cars, and certain leased assets, where the allowances are restricted, or where 100% first year allowances have not been claimed.

   **Separate Pool** includes all motor cars below an original cost of £8,000 which have been acquired since 1st June 1981, and certain leased assets which receive only restricted capital allowances.

   **Expensive Cars.** These are cars costing £8,000 or more. They should each be treated as if they had their own separate pool. The writing-down allowance is restricted to £2,000 per annum until the written-down value reaches £8,000 or below, and then a 25% allowance is available. If your business has several expensive cars, then each must be dealt with separately.

**Example**

| | | Allowance |
|---|---:|---:|
| Car Costs | £ 12,500 | |
| Year 1 | (2,000) | £ 2,000 |
| c/fwd | £ 10,500 | |
| Year 2 | (2,000) | £ 2,000 |
| | £ 8,500 | |
| Year 3 | (2,000) | £ 2,000 |
| | £ 6,500 | |
| Year 4    25% | (1,625) | £ 1,625 |
| | £ 4,875 | |
| Year 5    (Car Sale Proceeds) | (5,000) | |
| Balancing Charge | £ 125 | £ 125 |

2. Transfers of assets from an associated business (e.g. another business which you control), do not attract 100% first year allowances, only writing down allowances and these are added to the pool.
3. Motor Car additions have to be split between those above and below £8,000 and put in the appropriate column:
   Separate pool - cars below £8,000
   Expensive Cars - £8,000 and above
4. Disposal Proceeds are the actual proceeds from the sale of the asset, rather than the profit or loss, as entered in the profit and loss account. Cars disposed of which were acquired before 1st June 1980 may be deducted from the pool, rather than the separate pool.
5. **Balancing Charge or Allowance.** A balancing charge arises when you sell assets and the sales proceeds exceed the pool value. If the proceeds exceed original cost, then the balancing charge is restricted to original cost. Any balance over original cost is subject to Capital Gains Tax.

103

## Example

| | |
|---|---|
| Cost of asset | £ 500 |
| Allowances received | (400) |
| Pool c/fwd | 100 |
| Sales proceeds | 600 |
| Excess sales proceeds over pool value | £ 500 |
| Balancing charge = | £ 400 |
| Gain subject to Capital Gains Tax | £ 100 |

In practice, the original cost is not always known, and in the case of the sale of cars, no capital gain arises. A balancing charge, likewise, arises for separate pool cars and expensive cars, but in the latter case, the balancing charge has to be calculated on each car separately.

## Example

A balancing allowance arises in the case of the expensive cars, where the car is not fully written-off when it is sold and the proceeds do not exceed the tax written down value.

e.g.

| | |
|---|---|
| Cost | £ 12,500 |
| Written-off 3 years @ £2,000 | (6,000) |
| | £ 6,500 |
| Sales Proceeds | (5,000) |
| Balancing Allowance | £ 1,500 |

6. The writing-down allowance of 25% is based on the pool value after additions and disposals.
7. First Year Allowances are available on nearly all plant and machinery and commercial vehicles. The allowance has been 100% for many years, allowing capital purchases to be written-off in the year of purchase.
   In the 1984 Budget, Nigel Lawson announced various radical changes to the tax system which affected capital allowances.

The first year allowance is being phased out leaving only writing down allowances. The rates of allowance are:

| Periods to which rates apply | Rate of First Year Allowance |
|---|---|
| Prior to 13-3-84 | 100% |
| 14-3-84 – 31-3-85 | 75% |
| 1-4-85 – 31-3-86 | 50% |
| 1-4-86 – onwards | NIL |

However, in the 1985 Budget it was announced that on the phasing out of the first year allowances on 31st March, 1986, in certain circumstances a business would be able to elect to write off plant and machinery slightly faster than the 25% reducing balance basis. These circumstances are where the taxpayer expects to sell the equipment within five years for less than the tax written down value. An example would be computer equipment which only has a short life. The 25% reducing balance basis still applies to the cost of the separate piece of equipment, but a balancing charge or allowance is calculated for the equipment when it is sold rather than merging this with the pool assets. This has the effect of giving the allowances in full over the asset's life. If the asset is not sold within the five year period, then the written down value is added to the pool.

**Example:**

Asset purchased in 1987 for £1,000. Accounting date 31-12-87 sold in December 1989 for £500.

| | | |
|---|---|---:|
| y/e 31-12-87 | Cost | £1,000 |
| | WDA 25% | (250) |
| | | 750 |
| y/e 31-12-88 | WDA | (188) |
| | | 562 |
| Sales Proceeds | | (500) |
| Balancing Allowance | | £ 62 |

## 8. Private Use of Cars

If you use your car for your business and there is an element of private use, then, by agreement with the Revenue, a portion of the writing-down allowance, when calculated, will be disallowed, depending on the extent of the private use.

**Example**

|  | Car Cost | Disallowed say 15% | Capital Allowance Claimed |
|---|---|---|---|
|  | £ 7,500 |  |  |
| Year 1 WDA 25% | (1,875) | £ 281 | £ 1,594 |
| c/fwd | £ 5,625 |  |  |
| Year 2 WDA 25% | (1,406) | £ 211 | £ 1,195 |
| c/fwd | £ 4,219 |  |  |

## 9. Trade carried on for Less than One Year

If you carry on the trade for less than 1 year, then the writing-down allowances, but *not* the first year allowances, are restricted on a time apportioned basis for the length of period for which the trade is carried on.

e.g.  Year 1, 9 months trading
WDA = £1,250 – restricted to 9/12 = £937.50

# Appendix IV

*Industrial Buildings*

When you buy an industrial building which is new and has not received any allowances, the situation will be something similar to the computation shown below. The rates of initial and writing-down allowance will depend on the year of purchase. Recent Rates are given in the table below.

|  | Cost | Written Down Value B/fwd | Initial Allowance Say 50% | Writing Down Allowance 4% | Written Down Value C/fwd |
|---|---|---|---|---|---|
| Year 1 | 27,000 |  | 13,500 | 1,080 | 12,420 |
| Year 2 |  | 12,420 |  | 1,080 | 11,340 |
| Year 3 |  | 11,340 |  | 1,080 | 10,260 |

If the building was sold for say £30,000 there would be a balancing charge of £(27,000 − 10260) = £16,740. A balancing charge is treated like taxable income in the tax computation and added to the trading profit. The purchaser would receive the following writing-down allowance.

$$\frac{10,260 + 16,740}{(25 - 4)} = \frac{27,000}{21}$$

$$= £1,285 \text{ per annum}$$

i.e. There is no initial allowance and the building is written-off over the remainder of its life which is deemed to be 25 years. Four years have already gone.

If the building was sold at the end of year 4 for only £10,000, then the seller would receive a balancing allowance of £260 which is deducted from the taxable profit.

The buyer would receive allowances of:

$$\frac{10{,}000 + 260}{(25 - 4)} = £488 \text{ per annum}$$

*Recent Rates of Initial and Writing Down Allowances for Buildings*

| Date Expenditure Incurred | Rate of Initial Allowance | Rate of Writing Down Allowance |
|---|---|---|
| 13–11–74 – 10–3–81 | 50% | 4% |
| 11– 3–81 – 13–3–84 | 75% | 4% |
| 14– 3–84 – 31–3–85 | 50% | 4% |
| 1– 4–85 – 31–3–86 | 25% | 4% |
| 1–4–86 → | NIL | 4% |

# Appendix V

*Advance Corporation Tax*

Advance Corporation Tax (ACT) is payable whenever a dividend is paid and the fact that a dividend has been paid must be declared to the Revenue each quarter on a Return form CT61.

The quarters are ending:

31 March
30 June
30 September
31 December

The form has to be submitted together with any tax due 14 days following the end of the quarter i.e on 14th January for the quarter ending 31st December.

The rate of ACT depends on the basic rate of tax. When the rate of tax is 30% the ACT payable is $30/(100-30)$ x dividend actually paid i.e 3/7ths.

For example:

Dividend paid £70.

ACT 3/7 x 70 = 30.

In the hands of the shareholder who receives the dividend, he actually receives £70 and is deemed to have received £70 + £30 = £100 with £30 of tax already having been effectively deducted at source.

The amount of ACT which may be set-off against the corporation tax liability for each accounting period is restricted. The maximum ACT which may be set-off is the amount of ACT which would be payable in respect of a dividend payable at the end of the accounting period of an amount which together with the ACT thereon is equal to the income chargeable to corporation tax.

If the income chargeable to corporation tax was £1,000 then the ACT on a dividend of £700 would be £300 and the maximum set-off would be 300 i.e the basic rate of income tax. If the rate of corporation tax was say 40%, the CT payable on the profit would be £400, and of this up to £300 of ACT may be set-off. i.e rate of corporation tax minus basic rate of income tax must be left into charge. This is called mainstream corporation tax.

In any tax year, it may be that the rate of corporation tax and the rate of ACT are the same in which case there is no restriction. Any ACT which cannot be used is carried forward to the next accounting period, or carried back to the preceding six accounting periods.

# Appendix VI

*Sub-contractors in the Construction Industry*

If you think you might need a sub-contractor's certificate, or your operations are such that you think that you are hiring sub- contractors for part of your work, then we suggest you contact your local tax office and obtain the booklets IR14, IR15 and IR40. If you are unsure of your status, they will be able to give you advice. The following is an outline of when the scheme applies and the different types of certificates available.

In the construction industry a special tax deduction scheme applies instead of the PAYE scheme where any payments are made by contractors to sub-contractors. Some people may act only in one capacity, but others may act as both contractors and sub-contractors depending on their role in the overall construction operation. For example the site operator may hire an excavation company. In this instance the site operator is the contractor and the excavation company is the sub-contractor. The excavation company may in turn hire individuals to work for them who are not permanently on their payroll. These individuals are sub-contractors while the excavation company is the contractor.

**Operations within the Construction Industry covered by the scheme.**

The scope of the scheme is wide, and even extends to landscape gardening at the end of a project. As a general guide, the term covers almost anything done to a permanent or temporary building, structure, civil engineering work or installation including:

    site preparation
    construction
    alteration
    repair
    dismantling
    demolition

The following items are excluded:
  Work of architects, surveyors and consultants
  Signwriting, board installation and repair
  Installing security systems e.g. alarms
  Manufacture of components e.g. precast concrete slabs
  formed in a factory
  Drilling for oil or gas or extraction of minerals


## Outline of the scheme

When a contractor pays a sub-contractor he must check whether the sub-contractor has a sub-contractor's certificate issued by the Inland Revenue. If the sub-contractor does not have such a certificate, then the contractor must deduct tax from his payment to the sub-contractor, and pay the tax deducted to the Revenue. The rate of tax deduction is currently 30% i.e. the basic rate of tax. If the sub-contractor has a sub-contractor's certificate, then the contractor must check whether the certificate is valid, i.e. up to date and if it is an S certificate what value is shown on the certificate. The S certificate will show a weekly amount which the contractor may pay without deducting tax at source.

|  |  |
|---|---|
| For example, | |
| Weekly limit | £ 100 |
| Invoice/voucher issued | £ 200 |
| Materials included in voucher | £( 50) |
| | |
| Calculation of tax deduction | |
| Payment to be made | £ 200 |
| Less materials | £( 50) |
| | £ 150 |
| Less weekly limit | £(100) |
| | £ 50 |
| Tax on £50 @ 30% | £ 15 |
| Actual payment - £(200 − 15) | £ 185 |


## Obtaining a sub-contractor's certificate

The purpose of the certificate is to assist the Revenue in collection of tax. Where the Revenue are satisfied that the sub-contractor is submitting accounts and paying tax on a timely basis they will allow that sub-contractor to be paid without any tax being deducted at source. Where there is some doubt as to the sub-contractor's paying tax on all his profits then the Revenue insist that tax is deducted at source by the sub-contractor, and this tax is given as a credit against that person's eventual liability. The overall tax liability does not change, but without a certificate your cashflow will be adversely affected and in some instances the impact could be severe.

The issue of certificates is not as arbitrary as just outlined, there are strict rules laid down, and the sub-contractor has a right of appeal.

The conditions for obtaining a certificate are:-
1. You are working in the construction industry in the United Kingdom.
2. If you are just starting in business that you have a satisfactory record of employment.
3. You have a good record of paying your tax and national insurance.
4. You run your business properly, by this it is meant that you run the business from proper premises, you have a business bank account, and keep proper accounting records.

There are several types of certificate depending on the type of sub-contractor:-

| Type of Certificate | Colour | To Whom Issued |
| --- | --- | --- |
| 714 I | Yellow | Issued to an individual in business on his own. |
| 714 P | Red | Issued to an individual in a partnership, and to certain directors. |
| 714 P | Red | Issued to a company. |
| 714 C | Pink/Beige | Issued to larger companies not required to use vouchers. |
| 714 S | Green diagonal | Issued to certain individuals where there is a limit as to the amount which may be paid without deduction of tax. |

# Appendix VII

*Registration for VAT*

## 1. Compulsory Registration.

A trader who makes taxable supplies in excess of certain statutory registration limits and who is not exempt from registration by virtue of the fact that all the supplies are zero-rated is liable to compulsory registration.

If a trader is late in applying for registration, the registration takes effect from the date that registration should have been applied for. This can have severe consequences. VAT will have to be paid on all sales made from the date of registration irrespective of whether it has been charged or can be recovered from customers.

The statutory limits as announced in the Budget on 19th March, 1985 are.

| Period in force | Quarter Limit £ | Four Quarter Limit £ |
|---|---|---|
| 14-3-84 – 19-3-85 | 6,200 | 18,700 |
| 20-3-85 | 6,500 | 19,500 |

The quarter limit is applied in relation to the value of taxable supplies in a quarter, that is a three month period ending 31st March, 30th June, 30th September and 31st December. If the supplies exceed either the quarter or four quarter limit then the trader should register within 10 days of the end of the quarter in which the taxable turnover exceeds the limit, and registration should take effect within 21 days of the end of the quarter, or such earlier date as may mutually be agreed.

## 2. Voluntary Registration

A trader who makes taxable supplies who is not liable for compulsory registration may request to be registered and will thereafter be treated as if he were liable for registration. The grant of voluntary registration is at the discretion of the VAT commissioners.

The advantage of voluntary registration is that for a new business it means you can get the business established in a manner in which you expect to continue and you do not have to worry about checking turnover limits at the end of each quarter. Also registration gives the impression to customers that turnover is already above the registration limits which in certain circumstances may be beneficial.

3. **Deregistration.**

Deregistration is available where turnover limits fall below the registration limits, or where taxable supplies at the standard rate become zero-rated.

There are two tests to be applied, historical turnover limits and expected future turnover limits.

A registered person may deregister if his taxable supplies in each of the two year periods prior to the request are below the prescribed limit, and the taxable person was registered throughout the two year period and there are grounds for believing that the taxable supplies in the subsequent year will not exceed the future turnover limit.

| Period in Force | Historical Turnover | Future Turnover |
|---|---|---|
| 1-6-83 – 31-5-84 | 18,000 | 17,000 |
| 1-6-84 – 31-5-85 | 18,700 | 17,700 |
| 1-6-85 | 19,500 | 18,500 |